THE BIBLE I

THOUGHT

I KNEW

Peter B. Nagy

The journey to wisdom and greater understanding holds two potential pitfalls, not starting and not finishing.

Sadly, many invest much time in seminars, conferences and church attendance; but know less about Scripture than ever before. It is time that we, as congregations, understand our divine obligation to know the origins and history of what we actually believe in. Since Christianity is the continuation of the Jewish Religion, we should look to our Judaic legacy for Bible answers; and wean ourselves from Greco-Roman concepts and philosophy. Let us not examine Scripture through the lens of an institution.

To order additional copies or contact us:

Email: cainbridgeministries@comcast.net

Website: http://home.comcast.net/~psnagy/

2

This book is dedicated to the Lord, who provided the pleasant and kind woman responsible for maintaining a home filled with an attitude of thankfulness, cheerfulness, creativity, peace and encouragement. Without Him and her, this work would have never been possible.

INTRODUCTION

People will occasionally stumble upon the truth, and then pick themselves up and scurry off as though nothing ever happened.

Just as iron sharpens iron, we should study together to have our spiritual senses exercised; so all of us are ready and able to refute contradictions and unsound doctrine. Please join us for an intriguing adventure as we examine some Immaculate Misconceptions and scrutinize a few Great Omissions. Let's compare notes as we faithfully search together for firm Scriptural foundation amidst all the traditions and doctrines and confusion-Oh My!

It is not our intention to question the sincerity, salvation or anointing of anyone who may hold a different view on any topic. The purpose of our efforts is to provide some clarity on certain subjects, and to address familiar issues that continually surface in the average church group. When someone who is honestly mistaken hears the truth, they will either cease to be mistaken or they will cease to be honest.

Many believers are unaware of the layers of accumulated tradition practiced in church today, having little or no roots in Scripture. So, if you have been putting in the time to learn more about the Bible, allow us to share some information we found helpful and beneficial.

Not one topic in these pages changes anything in the Bible. Our information should only enhance what you already know and understand about the Bible. We should always be diligent to research and verify what is in this or any book we read. All the names, dates, places and verses are provided for reference and your consideration. Shalom and the Lord bless.

TABLE OF CONTENTS

Mary Magdalene a Prostitute?
Did Yeshua Carry the Cross?
Good Friday?
Shroud of Turin
God Heareth not Sinners?
By His Stripes, Are We Healed?
Were 120 People in an Upper Room?

Was Lucifer ever the Name of the Devil?
Christmas and Easter
Halloween
The Virgin Mary and Catholicism
Is the Cross a Christian Symbol?
Did Mary have other Children after Yeshua?

The Pre-Tribulation Rapture
The Day that No Man Knows
Sun Darkened, Blood Moon and Falling Stars
Absent from the Body, Present with the Lord?
The Parable of the Rich Man and Lazarus
Thief on the Cross

Trinity...The Forbidden Topic
Baptism in the Name of the Father, Son and Holy Spirit
God Appearing in Human Form
The Kingdom of God – Now or Future?
Unknown Tongues
Altar Calls
Slain in the Spirit
Secret Bible Codes
Da Vinci's Painting, the Last Supper

Questions and Answers

CHAPTER ONE

The Creation of Man

Here's what I thought I knew: Adam and Eve were the first humans, and they were told to go forth and multiply.

Here's more to consider: Either Adam and Eve were placed in a world that was already populated with all the various races, or they were created at the same time all the other races were. On the sixth day, God created all the different races of males and females around the world (Gen. 1:26-31); then rested the seventh day. Adam was created from dust and mist; and a garden was planted in the east part of a land called Eden, whether on, or after the sixth day. But, unlike the sixth day when both males and females were created; Adam was alone, naming animals, and couldn't find a suitable mate (Gen. 2:20). Eve was made later to join him, from a rib and not dust. It does not say Adam and Eve were told to go forth and multiply. When the first son Cain went to the neighboring land of Nod, he married a girl who was likely not his sister (Gen. 4:16, 17). Where did these other people come from?

The 2013 Jewish calendar is at 5774 years from Adam; which is about 3760 BC. China and Japan may have had agriculture, the wheel, and had domesticated animals by around 4000 BC; but neither of their uninterrupted histories includes being wiped out by Noah's flood (2200-2100 BC). Evidence indicates that South America, Australia, China, India, and all the races of people were living on their respective continents before, or at least by, the creation of Adam. Otherwise, wouldn't every battle in the Bible have been relatives against relatives? Isn't the Bible just a specialized account of a chosen people (descendants of Adam and Eve), to make the name of the Lord known throughout the world? Guess it worked, eh? This would explain how every distant nation, race and people were creating their own distinct and respective histories simultaneously with, or even previous to Adam and Eve.

Do Angels have Wings?

Here's what I thought I knew: Of course angels have wings; just look at all the pictures, paintings, movies and Valentine cards!

Here's more to consider: All the Bible references have angels appearing in male form with male names, but never in a female form. They are spirit beings that can appear discreetly in human form or they can make humans tremble; but are never described with wings. Would a spirit being need wings to fly?

Cherubim are not cute little fat babies with wings and a bow. They are described by Ezekiel as being ten cubits tall with four faces; four wings and a ten cubit wing span (Ezek. 10:1-22). They have a semblance of human hands, feet like a calf and a sparkling wheel within a wheel that seems to accompany them wherever they go (Ezek. 1:5-25). These creatures are not called angels.

Seraphim are beings described by Isaiah as having six wings and flying around the throne of the Lord saying, holy, holy, holy (Isa. 6:1-3). John describes six winged ones as covered with eyes and having four faces (Rev. 4:6-10). These beings are not called angels either. So, it turns out the common depiction of big fluffy, feathery wings on angels comes more from imagination and artistic license, than from any information the Bible actually provides.

A Global or Local Flood?

Here's what I thought I knew: The flood waters covered the planet, completely submerging Mt. Everest. Noah had every species and variety of animal, bird, reptile and insect on board the ark, as well as the food to feed them all for a year. All of nature today stems from these ark survivors; and all peoples today are descendants of Noah and his sons. It is even said that it never rained on earth until the time of the flood.

Here's more to consider: By examining this event, there is nothing that threatens our salvation or our faith in the Lord and the Bible. Yes, we believe the flood happened, so let's look the evidence for and against a universal, or a regional flood.

Some people say that God had not caused it to rain upon the earth until Noah and the flood. If we look at (Gen. 2:4-7), it says "before" there were herbs, plants and a man to till the ground; it had not rained upon the earth. It seems unlikely, once there were plants on earth and a man to till the ground; that for over 1,600 years the Lord withheld the life-giving mist or rain system that He designed and put in place for His creation. There is no question a vast inundation did take place in the plains of Iraq and the Persian Gulf. The date the flood ended is recorded by Josephus as the 17th day of Nisan (Antiquities of the Jews, book 1, 3:5), which would be around 2100-2200 BC, and 1,657 years from Adam; which incidentally is the same day Messiah rose from the grave, three days after Passover.

Should the earth and Mt. Everest been submerged, (which would require over five miles of water) the water level and the ark would have been at around 29,000 feet in altitude. That would have provided cold temperatures for desert and jungle animals, as well as people to endure for months. What about the lack of oxygen at that altitude? Mountaineers call anything above 26,000 feet the "death zone" because there is not enough oxygen to sustain human life. Would the water have frozen at that temperature and height? If the ark were to rest on mountains of that height as the water receded a few thousand feet; wouldn't the water level only be down to 20,000 or 25,000 feet? How did a dove bring back an olive branch, if olive trees usually thrive from sea level up to about 3,000 feet in altitude?

One of the wettest places on earth is in Hawaii, which receives almost 500 inches of rainfall per year. For the rain to cover Mt. Everest in forty days, the worldwide rainfall would have exceeded 8,700 inches per day! It is figured to require approximately eight times the water now available on the planet to bring the water level up to cover Mt. Everest. This would not be fresh water, but an 8 to 1 mix of fresh to saltwater.

9

Most salt and freshwater fish would not survive the mix. The people on the ark could not drink this mixture; which would make them have to store a year's worth of fresh water for them and the animals. This would not be a problem if the flood had been freshwater covering a regional area.

Some aquatic life dies with just a few degrees of temperature change. The majority of marine life lives in the upper 1,000 ft. of the ocean. The depth pressure underneath five miles of sea is well over 12,000 lbs. psi. There are few species that can survive this pressure. And where did eight times the water we see today go after the flood? Why don't the lakes and glaciers exhibit this salt and freshwater mix now?

We must ask how all the different species of fish found their way back to their respective and remote habitats, and specialized environments. After floating five miles above the earth for up to a year, how did the ark land right back in the same region it started from, and not some other distant location on earth?

The trees and vegetation on the whole planet must be considered. Being five miles underwater for up to a year, at pressures over 12,000 lbs. psi; would have killed most, if not all plant life. It would also cut off all sunlight, and the earth would have had complete darkness for up to a year. How would any of the plant kingdom have survived to produce the next season's seeds; without a year of light to grow the seeds? A local flood does not have this dilemma.

We must also wonder not only how animals, birds, insects and reptiles would have traveled to the ark, but how they would have returned to their respective lands, islands and habitats. Australia has life found in no other place on earth, and this is no exception. Many areas have life not found in any others.

There are tens of thousands of different insects, snails, slow moving animals and reptiles. In the amount of time it would have taken for them to migrate over land, deserts, mountains, lakes, rivers, oceans and glaciers; their lifespan would have dictated they would have had to reproduce numerous times

10

during their pilgrimage to the ark. This would also be necessary for the return trip to their respective habitats after the flood. This problem is solved with a local flood of the 45,000 square mile area of Mesopotamia, and local animals on the ark.

There would have been some insects with lifespans much less than the year they spent on the ark, so they would have had to reproduce on the ark. Reptiles like insects to eat, which would require extra insects. Noah was instructed to take food on the ark for the people and the animals (Gen. 6:21). Some animals eat other animals for food, which would require extra animals to feed the lions and tigers and bears...oh my. Some animals eat fish, which would require a constant supply of fresh fish. Some insects eat other insects, which would require extra other insects for the food chain. Anteaters would need many ants.

Not only is the weight on the ark from one or seven pair of all the animals on earth unimaginable, but the weight of the amount of food required to feed every species on the planet for a year is mind-boggling. Two African and two Indian elephants can weigh 40,000 lbs. The food needed just for these four animals could be over 200,000 lbs. for a year! There was seven pair of some animals; of which 14 cattle can eat 250,000 lbs. of hay and silage in one year. Then there are rhinos, pandas, polar bears, wolverine, jaguar, ocelot, giraffes, water buffalo, bison, every kind of deer, elk, antelope, oxen, moose, cow, sheep, goat, weasel, mice, dogs, cats, tortoise, kangaroo, koala, wombat, toucan, anaconda, python, cobra, cockatoo, hyena, platypus, penguins, frogs, monkeys and vultures; all with different and specialized diets. The amount of food every species required for a year surely could have exceeded one million pounds and would have been more than eight people could have kept up with, not only collecting and storing beforehand, but feeding the animals daily for a year. The amount of manure produced daily from every species on earth, would also have been a full time chore. The weight of all the species on earth would easily exceed one million pounds, to add to the million pounds of food. A smaller group of local animals and a local flood avoids these difficulties.

11

Depending on the measure of a cubit; if the 450 ft. ark was Noah's first boat, then he and his sons did very well with primitive tools. With centuries of experience building the finest ocean going vessels, even with steel reinforcements; teams of wooden ship building experts today, have difficulty building a wood boat that exceeds 300-350 feet. Wood ships of this size flex, break apart and sink; and have not served well even in calm seas. One large wood ship of this size, without cargo, broke apart and sank, while being towed to another location!

The Genesis account of the flood uses the translated word "earth." Depending on how the Hebrew word "erets" (land, ground, country or earth) is translated, the understanding can change a bit. If the Lord flooded the "land" or "country" in which Noah dwelt, it would have wiped out the wickedness in the Mesopotamian region and not necessarily wiped out the planet. This was before the people were dispersed and the languages were changed (Gen. 11:5-9). If all people had been killed by the flood, how could there be the kingdoms of Babylon, Erech, Akkad, Calneh and Assyria already up and running in just two generations for Nimrod (Gen. 10:9-12) to conquer and rule? These were established civilizations that seemingly were not interrupted by the flood; and there had not been enough time for these various cities and peoples to have descended from Ham, Shem and Japheth.

At the time when Abram went to Egypt, it was an ancient civilization that had not been wiped out by the flood. The oldest recorded calendar date from Egypt is around 4200 BC, but the oldest Jewish biblical date is about 3760 BC. Museum pieces from China, Japan and India seem to pre-date Noah; and these cultures do not appear to have been wiped out by a flood. In a time when most people did not travel more than 100 miles from where they were born, do you think Noah was aware that Japan, North and South America, or Australia even existed in his day?

If Noah was the descendant of Seth, we must also wonder about the other lineage of Cain. Jabal was the first to live in tents and raise cattle, Jubal was the first to play the harp and flute, and Tubal-Cain made tools out of bronze and iron (Gen. 4:19-22).

Were these people killed by the flood, along with their respective talents? Did the Bronze Age come to a wet screeching halt until the art of metal working was rediscovered after the flood? Did music and musical instruments become nonexistent until someone after the flood invented them again? If all people today are descendants of Noah and his three sons; that would mean Noah had a white son, a brown son and a black son. Wouldn't Noah have looked suspiciously at Mrs. Noah? We must also wonder with whom did Ham, Shem and Japheth's children marry and have families?

Historians such as Berosus the Chaldean, Nicolaus of Damascus and Flavius Josephus speak of the ark being within access of people. Josephus said; many who fled to Mt. Baris at the time of the Deluge were saved (Antiquities of the Jews, book 1, 3:6). He added; Noah's three sons were the first to descend from the mountains into the plains of Shinar and persuaded "others" who were afraid of lower grounds for fear of another flood (Antiquities of the Jews, book 1, 4:1). Who were these "others," who were afraid to leave higher ground to go and live on the plains? It was not thought of as a global flood 2,000 years ago.

Yes, sea shell fossils are found at high altitudes, but less than a year of flood would not be enough time for those massive amounts of shell upon shell growth to take place before the water began to recede back to normal. The Scripture gives record of the rate at which the water receded, at least for a period of time. The water went down at least 15 cubits in 150 days (Gen. 7:20; 8:3-5). If the water had covered Mt. Everest; it would take over 200 years at this rate, to get back to normal. Yet, it took less than a year.

There is a DNA test that is supposed to tell if a person has Jewish heritage going back to Abraham. Since Abraham is the descendent of Noah, anyone from Noah's lineage through Ham, Shem and Japheth should test positive for this Jewish DNA gene. Wouldn't that also include all the Arab descendants from Ishmael (Abraham and Hagar) who should test positive for the Abrahamic gene too? Wouldn't all the generations of people who came from Abraham's remarriage and six other children

13

after Sarah died (Gen 25: 1-4) also test positive? This invites the logical conclusion that someone testing "negative" for this Jewish gene going back to Noah, would mean their lineage came from people who were not wiped out by a global flood.

As a regional event, the types of local vegetation quickly grew and the animals also migrated back into the wasted area so that after a period of time, the damaging effects of the flood were eliminated. These are the strongest points to us that would indicate a regional event. Although God can do anything, the evidence seems to support the smaller scale deluge rather than the magnitude of a global flood. We are here now; however the flood occurred should not cause contention between believers.

Where is Noah's Ark?

Here's what I thought I knew: Noah's ark is somewhere on Mt. Ararat, at an elevation of about 14,000 feet.

Here's more to consider: The ark came to rest on the mountains (plural) of Ararat (Gen. 8:4). All the lower hills surrounding Mt. Ararat are called the "mountains" of Ararat. Noah sent a dove that returned with an olive branch in its beak. Beside a dove being a very short distance flyer, olive trees seem to grow best from sea level, up to about 3,000 ft. in altitude. Noah had one or more pair of animals on the ark. How would clumsy sheep, cows, camels and most other animals find their way down from a place 14,000 ft. in elevation, which we cannot even access today, with all our advanced equipment and technology?

There is a city in Armenia called Naxuana or Nakhichevan, which claims Noah's tomb. The name means "here Noah settled." In reference to the arks' location, Berosus the Chaldean said, "A part of the ship was still in Armenia and people were taking pieces for amulets to avert mischief." Nicolaus of Damascus made mention: "the remains of the timber were a great while preserved." Historian Josephus said "many who fled to Mt Baris at the time of the Deluge were saved"

(Antiquities of the Jews, book 1, 3:6). These accounts place the ark within access of people, and the flood was remembered as regional, not worldwide.

How many Animals on the Ark?

Here's what I thought I knew: Noah took seven pair of every clean beast and one pair of every kind of unclean beast.

Here's more to consider: Noah took seven pair of every beast that was clean, seven pair of birds of the air and one pair of the animals that are "not clean" (Gen. 7:2, 3). The term "not clean" has nothing to do with the term "unclean" in the food laws dictated by the Torah (Law of Moses). This was centuries before Moses, and before the Torah was even written.

The term "not clean" in this passage meant "unsuitable for sacrifice." The only five acceptable sacrifices mentioned in the Bible are sheep, goats, cattle (oxen), pigeons and doves. Remember, a year after the flood, every moving thing that lives was acceptable for food, as long as the blood was drained (Gen. 9:3, 4). It would be centuries later, when the unclean food laws would be instituted in the wilderness.

120 Years to Build the Ark?

Here's what I thought I knew: It took 120 years to build the ark.

Here's more to consider: The Bible does not say it took 120 years to build the ark. There is a verse that says, "The Lord said His Spirit shall not always strive with man...his days shall be 120 years" (Gen. 6:3).

Noah did not begin to have children until he was 500 years old (Gen. 5:32). When God instructed Noah to build the ark, his sons were already grown and married (Gen. 6:10, 18). The Bible does not say how long it took to build the ark. But, if he

15

started building it after his sons were grown and married, then sailed when he was 600; it took them less than 100 years to build the ark.

Generational Curse

Here's what I thought I knew: Some sources indicate Ham means "dark or swarthy one." When Noah pronounced a curse on Ham, it meant that all his descendants (dark people) were destined and doomed to be subservient and slaves for all time.

Here's more to consider: First of all, according to the Hebrew speaking scholars I know, the name "Ham" (Cham) does not mean hot, scorched or burnt. This definition came from questionable origins (white men trying to justify slavery). Second, if Noah was the father of three sons who repopulated the earth; wouldn't this curse be affecting approximately one third of the current earth's population? Third, Noah did not curse Ham. Noah said, "Cursed be thy son Canaan, for he shall be a servant to his brothers" (Gen. 9:25). This surely was not a curse on every descendant of Canaan until the end of time.

Was this a more damaging punishment to Ham than a simple scolding? To have his son's whole life compromised because of one little indiscretion? Simply, Canaan was to take a back seat to, or be a servant to his brothers. At least he was with family. You can trace the lineage of Canaan and find that many of his descendants were wealthy with fine linens, land, gold, silver, precious jewels; and they even had slaves of their own! Another point to ponder, everyone is responsible for his own behavior and sin. A father's guilt is not put upon his son, and the son's guilt is not put upon his father (Ezekiel Chapter 18).

No Feeble People?

Here's what I thought I knew: Due to forty years of miraculous, supernatural and divine healing, there was not one feeble person among the Israelites, when God brought them out of the wilderness. Here is the verse used for a proof text: "He brought them forth also with silver and gold, and there was not one feeble person among their tribes" (Psalms 105:37).

Here's more to consider: First of all, the verse is about them coming out of Egypt, and not the wilderness forty years later! If we turn to the actual story we find: "Remember what Amalek did unto thee by the way, when ye were come forth out of Egypt. How he met thee by the way, and smote the hindmost of thee, even all that were feeble behind thee, when thou wast faint and weary; and he feared not God" (Deut. 25:17, 18).

The biblical account informs us that the faint, weary and feeble people were killed in battle. This is why there were no feeble people, and not due to miraculous healing. We know that there were some healings in the wilderness (Num. 12:10-15; 21:9). But, there were some that did not get healed. There were lepers, those who had an issue and those who had been defiled by the dead (Num. 5:1-4). These were commanded to be put out of the camp. They had not been miraculously healed.

There were the blind, lame, those with a blemish, crookbacked, those with scurvy, scabbed, broken footed or broken handed, etc. (Lev. 19:14) (Lev. 21:17-21). These afflictions received no miraculous healing. Keep in mind, only two people from the original group (that left Egypt) were allowed to enter into the Promised Land. The rest died at some point during the forty years, being replaced by descendants. Death is hardly proof of miraculous health.

Only Manna for 40 Years?

Here's what I thought I knew: The Israelites only had manna to eat for forty years; with the exception of some quail. The Lord provided all their nutritional needs with only manna.

Here's more to consider: The Israelites were commanded to eat

17

the Passover meal every year on the fourteenth day of the first month (Lev. 23:5). There was an allowance for a second Passover meal one month later if someone missed the first one due to an unclean condition (Num. 9:10-12). The Passover meal was lamb, bitter herbs and unleavened bread; so once a year they were supposed to eat meat, herbs and bread (Num. 9:5).

The term "unleavened bread" is used so directly, it lets us know they could make "leavened bread" (Exod. 12:5-10). Yeast is specifically mentioned as being available (Lev. 6:17).

We know the Israelites had with them cattle, goats, sheep, turtledoves and pigeons for the entire 40 years (Lev. 1:2-14). Did you notice the terms (Exod. 12:38) "herds and flocks" and (Deut. 3:19) "very much cattle"? We could also presume, besides the meat that the livestock and poultry provided, there would have been eggs, milk, butter, and cheese available as well (Num. 32:1). There were cakes and wafers (Lev. 2:4) made with fine flour, oil, salt, corn and honey (Lev. 2:11-14).

How did they make bread? They had pans, griddles and ovens for baking (Lev. 7:9). Do you really think they had cooking utensils and various foods they could cook, and only ate manna for forty years? The children of Israel are commanded not to eat any manner of "fat" of oxen, sheep or goat (Lev. 7:23). Why would they be instructed to remove the fat, if they were not going to eat the remaining meat?

Eating of animals that died of whatever cause, or one killed by other beasts was forbidden; but they could sell it to a stranger (Deut. 14:21). This command shows their access to hunt a variety of wild beasts natural to the region (Lev. 7:24). Any fowl or beast bagged by the hunt, which was lawful to eat, must have the blood removed before consumption (Lev. 17:13). Why would they be instructed to drain the blood, if they were not going to eat the remaining meat?

The conditions when taking a Nazarite vow include: abstaining from wine and strong drink, vinegar of wine, vinegar of strong drink and liquor of grapes (Num. 6:2-4). Nor could they eat moist grapes, dried grapes or anything made from the vine tree, from the kernels to the husk. Wouldn't the items they were to abstain from imply they "were" eating and drinking these things, when not taking a Nazarite vow?

There is mention of oil, flour, grain, yeast and the animal sacrifices for the Levite priests to consume (Lev. 6:15-17). We also know the priests were instructed to and did eat meat and bread from the sacrifices (Lev. 8:31). Somehow, I do not get the impression that all they had to eat was manna.

They were given instructions about tithing grain, crops from the land, fruit from trees and every "tenth" animal that passed under the rod (Lev. 27:30-34). How could they tithe grain, crops, fruit from trees and every tenth animal, if all they had to eat was manna? How did the priests pay tithes of food or eat of the grain, bread and meat for forty years (Num. 18:21-32) if the Israelites didn't tithe of their foods?

Wine and wheat are mentioned (Num. 18:12). The scouts brought back grapes, pomegranates and figs from their trip into Canaan (Num. 13:23). There are grapes and grain mentioned (Deut. 23:24, 25). When in the land of Esau, the Lord instructed them to go and "buy" meat to eat and water to drink (Deut. 2:6). It is very possible they even cultivated a few crops from time to time. He reminds them for forty years they lacked nothing (Deut. 2:7).

It is probable the Israelites traded with desert nomads and people of the land they were in. They even obtained cattle as spoils of battle (Deut. 2:35). If they obtained spoils of battle, wouldn't that indicate there were other people available to battle with, or trade with?

Manna (which means either: what is this? Or, it is manna) was given as a daily supplement while they were in the wilderness. It stopped falling when they entered into the Promised Land. Surely the Lord could make manna meet all the nutritional needs of the Israelites, but many verses in Scripture disprove the idea that manna was their "only" food for forty years.

Indestructible Shoes and Clothes?

Here's what I thought I knew: For forty years in the wilderness, the shoes and clothes of the Israelites miraculously never wore out. The verses used to substantiate this teaching are:

"Thy raiment waxed not old upon thee, neither did thy foot swell these forty years" (Deut. 8:4). "And I have led you forty years in the wilderness. Your clothes are not waxen old upon you, and thy shoe is not waxen old upon thy foot" (Deut. 29:5).

"Yea, forty years didst thou sustain them in the wilderness; so that they lacked nothing; their clothes waxed not old and their feet swelled not..." (Neh. 9:21).

Here's more to consider: Were their clothes and shoes supernaturally preserved? Or, is this just one more account of the Lord supplying all their needs, no matter what the need? We read that the Israelites had plenty of clothes and change of garments when they left Egypt (Exod. 12:34, 35). They carried their own clothes upon their shoulders and had even borrowed raiment from the Egyptians.

We know the sheep, goats, oxen and cattle would provide a constant supply of materials for the making of shoes and clothes. We also know they had craftsmen skilled in all manner of workmanship. They were able to fashion the gold, silver, brass and wood items that made up the Temple. They also made the veil in the Temple.

They were rather accomplished brick makers and bricklayers at their last employment in Egypt. There were engravers in stone, who made the priest's breastplate (Exod. 31:1-11). They were living in tents, so there had to be tentmakers.

Weaving and clothes making skills are apparent when the Lord told them to make the priest's garments (Exod. 28:3-10, 15). "And these are the garments which they shall make: a breastplate, an ephod, a robe, and a broidered coat, a mitre and a girdle of fine twined linen." They were also able to make breeches of linen (Exod. 28:42). There is no doubt they had all the supplies and craftsmanship to make new clothes and shoes.

The Lord gave them guidelines forbidding the mixture of various materials such as wool and linen together (Deut. 22:11). Why would the Lord instruct them on how to make their clothes in such a specific manner, if they were not making their clothes?

Of course, there were no J.C. Penny or K-mart stores to purchase new clothes at the time, so most people had to rely on their own craftsmanship. We cannot rule out the possibility of trade with the Moabites and other nomadic tribes either. They even had obtained spoils of war (Deut. 2:34-36).

What about over 600,000 children who were born and grew to adulthood during the forty year journey? Were infants miraculously born with clothing and shoes? Did the outfits that fit the infants, magically expand as the child matured? Did the shoes also miraculously stretch as their feet grew? Or, were there always enough supplies and materials to make replacements?

We must also think of damage to the clothing like an accidental rip or tear. Was the material wear proof? Didn't anybody wear a hole in the elbow or knee area of their garment for forty years? Did every sandal hold up and never break a strap?

Nehemiah states that for the forty years in the wilderness, they lacked nothing (Neh. 9:21).

It seems quite obvious, that the Lord God of Israel never let their garments grow old upon them for lack of replacements. Nor did He let their feet become swollen and bruised from worn out shoes. He provided for all their needs by supplying all the necessary materials in abundance.

Was Moses Slow of Speech?

Here's what I thought I knew: Because of the incident at the burning bush, when Moses tried to avoid being sent back to Egypt; some think of Moses as a stammering, stuttering, meek and wimpy kind of a guy.

Here's more to consider: Moses was only trying to avoid returning to Egypt. Moses first tried to avoid Egypt by asking God, "who am I that I should go before Pharaoh?" (Exod. 3:11). Then Moses asked, "what if I go to Israel and they ask me what God's name is?" (Exod. 3:13). Then Moses indicated the Israelites would not believe him or believe the Lord had appeared to him (Exod. 4:1). His claim to be slow of speech was his fourth and last attempt to avoid Egypt (Exod. 4:10-17).

He did repeat this slow of speech excuse a couple more times, but Moses' statements are the only evidence lending to this idea about a slow of speech speaking problem (Exod. 6:12, 30). Perhaps after living in a different land for 40 years, his memory of the Egyptian language was a little rusty.

Side Note: Did you know that God was about to kill Moses before he had even met up with Aaron (Exod. 4:24-26) to begin the Exodus into the wilderness? God was fulfilling a great promise to deliver all of Israel and it seems Moses hadn't even bothered to circumcise his own son. His wife didn't approve!

Who did most of the talking when they went before Pharaoh? Moses did. Aaron was there and surely he was not silent. It does say "they" spoke to Pharaoh in a couple passages. There is no indication of Moses having any difficulty speaking to Pharaoh a number of different times, nor did he ever "need" Aaron to speak for him.

A withdrawn kind of a guy is not the product of being raised as royalty (son of Pharaoh's daughter). Certainly, from this position, Moses acquired some manner of authority.

A hesitant kind of a guy is not the victor of battles as the general of Egypt's army (Antiquities of the Jews, book 2, 10:2). A wimpy kind of a guy does not kill an Egyptian guard who is not only trained for combat, but controls and commands many slaves under him (Exod. 2:12).

A timid kind of a guy does not go before Pharaoh (king of Egypt) and demand he release close to a million people that Egypt has ruled for generations.

A stay in the back kind of a guy does not command the Israelite army in battle for many years (Deut. 2:34-36). He had experience as a military leader from years ago in Egypt. A stammering kind of a guy does not lead close to a million people for 40 years in the wilderness.

A hesitant type of a guy does not break the Ten Commandments in a furious rage, and scold about 1,000,000 people. Was he slow of speech then?

I'm sure we could come up with many more feats that prove Moses was not a Casper Milquetoast kind of a guy. When Scripture refers to Moses as "meek," it is talking about him being "humble" and submission before God; not about him being timid.

Stephen said, "Moses was mighty in his words and his deeds" (Acts 7:22). There is no mention of any speech impediment anywhere in the Bible, other than when Moses tried to avoid going back to Egypt. Why was Moses so hesitant to go back? Having been mighty at leading the army of Egypt, Moses had felt the calling to free his people 40 years previous. He thought his people would recognize this calling; they didn't (Acts 7:25).

Did you notice that God sent Moses (Acts 7:35) as a "ruler and deliverer"? This is hardly a stammering, stuttering, slow of speech and wimpy occupation.

Joshua's Longest Day

Here's what I thought I knew: While Joshua was fighting the battle at Gibeon, the sun stopped in the sky for an extra day without moving. There was also a story about a space probe that couldn't be launched because they were missing 23 hours and 20 minutes out of elapsed time as a result of this event.

Here's more to consider: There is no record in the Bible or in history that the sun did not go down one day. Wouldn't the other half of the earth have had an extra day of darkness? There is absolutely no record of that in the Bible at all, or in history either. How would they possibly know how long the sun stayed in one place, if it did not move? The sun was the way they told time back then! Is the intended meaning of "about a whole day," a 12 hour day from dawn to dark, or a 24 hour day?

It may not mean the sun stopped, it could be the "sun stayed." How can the sun "stay" in the sky and hasten not to go down to the earth? The Hebrew word for sun can mean: the sun itself, the light from the sun, the heat from the sun or even a sunbeam. The word "day" at the end of (Josh. 10:13) means: to be hot, a day (#3117, Strong's Concordance). The normally hot day when the moon is over the Ajalon valley at midday is July 22 (International Standard Bible Encyclopedia, Vol. 1, p. 449). With this in mind, let's examine the story.

Don't forget, it is not actually the sun that would stop in the sky, but "the earth" would have to stop rotating in order to accomplish this. The earth rotates at 1,065 mph at the equator. The earth stopping would throw lakes, seas and rivers out of their beds. It would topple trees and crumble mountains, also causing earthquakes and volcanoes from the global stress.

Did the Lord stop the whole solar system just for this one battle? Another thing to consider is God's very integrity is expressed by the unceasing progression of day and night (Gen. 8:22). If we can stop the sun and moon from their established cycle, "then" we can break a Covenant with God (Jer. 33:20, 21). Joshua was more or less tricked into an alliance. After being awake all day, Joshua and his men were notified they were needed for battle. They had to march uphill all night long (about 20 miles and 3,000 ft. elevation gain) hauling all their battle gear. Would these tired men benefit from another 12 or 24 hours of day time in hot weather so they could win this battle? Joshua wanted this battle over quickly, as in a day.

Israel was winning the battle with great slaughter (Josh. 10:10). The enemy was fleeing and the Lord cast down hailstones that killed more than the swords (Josh. 10:11). In order to make hailstones large enough to kill a man, a storm has to have winds (up high) in excess of 100 mph. What part of the sun can stay in the sky (Josh. 10:13) and not go down to the earth? The storm provided the relief from the heat of the sun, that "stayed in the midst of heaven and hastened not to go down (to earth) about a whole day."

With a storm like that, could they even tell if the sun moved or not? The light of the sun and the moon would have been blocked and wouldn't "have gone down" to earth for about the whole day.

The miracle in this case, was not that the sun never moved in the sky. There was no day like that, before or after, because the Lord hearkened unto the voice of a man (Josh 10:14). Joshua did not ask in prayer or request, but in command, as though all of creation was at his disposal. The Lord made the battle over quickly, even in a day.

Of course, if there were to have been a "one day" time change in Joshua's day, that would put the Saturday Sabbath one day off for every week ever since! Surely this cannot be the case.

Back in 1984 I heard a story, now proven false. Supposedly, a space probe couldn't be launched because they were missing a day in elapsed time. They tried to attribute 23 hours and 20 minutes (about a whole day) to the time of Joshua's battle, so the probe wouldn't be off course. Using the Bible, they reportedly discovered the missing time was from Joshua's era; then they were able to launch the probe. Do you really believe this? Wouldn't there actually have been an "extra" day of time?

How can we know today if the earth stopped spinning about 3,500 years ago? The best we can do now is, observe the known paths of astrological bodies as we see them now. With this kind of time change theory, we could say the earth stopped rotating any number of times in history past, without a shred of evidence to back it up. Anyway, the fact that it was "extra" time and not "missing" time also tends to discredit this rumor.

Hezekiah's Shadow on a Sun Dial

Here's what I thought I knew: Supposedly even today, we are missing 40 minutes out of elapsed time, because the sun went back ten steps or degrees on the sun dial. If this is figured at four minutes to a degree, it would equal 40 minutes.

Here's more to consider: First of all, it was not a sun dial. The sun dial was not even invented until about six hundred years later. Some translations use the word "staircase." This would be the more accurate rendering. The shadow retreated ten steps on the staircase of Ahaz (2 Kings 20:11).

Does it actually say the sun moved in the sky? Or, is this simply a case where only the "shadow" moved backward on the staircase of Ahaz, from where it had already progressed to? The shadows from every other object remained the same, while the shadow moved on the staircase alone.

The Bible does not say that the sun moved. The Bible does not say there was any change in elapsed time. Isaiah makes no mention of any time change in his account (Isa. 38:7-9).

Remember, in order for this to take place, it is not the sun that moves in the sky, but the earth would have to stop rotating and then turn backwards. Then it would have to stop again and start turning in the normal direction again. Then it would have to progress even faster than usual for a while, to catch up to where it would have been if this had not taken place.

This would topple trees, crumble mountains and throw lakes, rivers and oceans out of their beds. Not only once would this have happened, but twice! There is absolutely no record of that in the Bible, or in history either.

Letters and a present were sent to Hezekiah because they heard he had been healed and had been given fifteen more years to live (Isa. 39:1). If there had been an actual change in time, wouldn't that deserve mention as much or more than just being healed from boils? The same story is repeated with absolutely no mention of any change in time (2 Chron. 32:31).

How did they come up with 40 minutes? Since it wasn't a sun dial but a staircase, 10 steps on a staircase has no relation to a time frame of 40 minutes. If it were 40 minutes to get the shadow to retreat ten steps, wouldn't it take another 40 minutes to catch back up to where it would have been? That would add up to 80 minutes; unless the earth went twice as fast as usual for a while, and then slowed to its normal speed.

Did the Lord find it necessary to halt the whole solar system and make it go backwards just to assure one guy that he would be healed of boils and live fifteen more years?

The same space launch story was also attributed to Joshua's longest day. Supposedly, after finding the 23 hours and 20 minutes, the space probe couldn't be launched because they were still missing 40 minutes in elapsed time. The probe would be off course if they could not find where the missing 40 minutes was from. They reportedly used this event with Hezekiah and the shadow to identify where the missing time had been lost and were able to launch their space probe successfully. Does this sound feasible to you?

As with the story from Joshua's battle, would there have been "missing" time, or would there have been "extra" time?

27

Did Ravens feed Elijah?

Here's what I thought I knew: It might have been people who fed Elijah meat and bread at the Kerith Ravine (1 Kings 17:4-6). Some notable scholars say the Hebrew word that is translated "ravens," could also be translated merchants, Arabians or men from a city named Arabah/Orbo (Josh. 18:18). In the book of Ezekiel, a contracted form of this word is translated "merchandise" (Ezek. 27:9, 27).

Here's more to consider: At first glance, it does not seem probable that a Jewish prophet would accept or consume meat and bread from a raven. A raven was classified as a scavenger and a detestable unclean bird according to the Torah (Law of Moses) (Lev. 11:13-15).

But, sometimes the simplest answer is the best answer. The Hebrew scholars that I know seem to agree it was ravens, meaning black (1 Kings 17:4). The Lord commanded Elijah to be at the ravine, the Lord commands the clouds (Isa. 5:6) and the locusts (2 Chron. 7:13), why not the ravens?

But, it does beg the inquiry; did the ravens drop off raw meat? Or did they have a way to cook the meat first? Did the ravens also have a way to measure and mix the ingredients, and to bake the bread? How would the ravens have had daily access to these food items? Wouldn't it be ironic if the ravens actually stole the meat and bread from Ahab and Jezebel's very table!

We admit the logic of some men who had not bowed the knee to Baal and having been commanded to feed Elijah is appealing. They could have been trusted not to disclose the prophet's location while he kept a low profile at the ravine. But, the Bible still says ravens/carrion.

Was this a symbolic lesson for the prophet, that he was being sustained by unclean messengers bringing unclean provisions? Was this an example of Israel being sustained by Jezebel's unclean Baal messengers bringing unclean doctrines? I think they could eat food carried by horse or camel, even though the animals themselves were unclean for eating. I wasn't there but, it sounds like he was eating less than desirable food from unknown sources being delivered by unclean birds, doesn't it?

Mount Carmel, How many Priests and Prophets?

Here's what I thought I knew: Elijah was challenging four hundred Baal priests and prophets, perhaps four hundred fifty, at the showdown on Mount Carmel.

Here's more to consider: Simple addition says there were four hundred fifty prophets of Baal, and four hundred prophets of Asherah (groves) for a grand total of eight hundred fifty priests and prophets (1 Kings 18:19). Doesn't Elijah going up against 850 priests and prophets make the event even more impressive?

He was not very politically correct when he razzed the priests and prophets about their god sleeping, being on a journey or "stepping aside," (1 Kings 18:27) which at the time meant "going to the bathroom." Elijah later had all eight hundred fifty of them slain (1 Kings 18:40).

Foot Race Against a Chariot?

Here's what I thought I knew: Elijah foot raced King Ahab's chariot from the showdown at Mount Carmel to Jezreel. Being older in years, he actually outran the chariot (1 Kings 18:46).

Here's more to consider: What does it mean when Elijah girded up his loins and ran before Ahab to the entrance of Jezreel? Does the terminology "ran before Ahab" mean they were racing, and Elijah won? There is no doubt the Lord could speed a person up so as to outrun a chariot. But, is this the intended meaning? Was the king out driving his chariot alone? Would the king be out driving his chariot without the usual group of soldiers for protection? Did the soldiers keep up with the chariot everywhere the king went? Weren't kings usually accompanied by an entourage? It was common in those days for a group of chanters to walk or "run" in front of a king's chariot, announcing his arrival, singing his praises and reciting his great deeds (1 Sam. 8:11) (2 Sam. 15:1).

The king's chariot usually had the best and fastest horses. Did all these chanters "outrun" the king's chariot also? Or, did Elijah simply join the group of chanters in front of King Ahab's chariot and "run" along with them to the entrance of Jezreel?

Chariot of Fire?

Here's what I thought I knew: Elijah was taken away on a chariot of fire and went straight up to heaven without dying.

Here's more to consider: The horses and chariot of fire merely separated Elisha and Elijah. Elijah went up by a whirlwind into heaven (2 Kings 2:11). There were fifty strong men who went to search for Elijah in case he had been cast on some mountain or in a valley. They searched for three days expecting to find him (2 Kings 2:16-18).

If Elijah had been taken "straight up" to heaven, would the fifty strong men have gone looking for him? How would they know which direction to begin looking, if had he been taken straight up? Or did they go searching, because they saw him carried away by a whirlwind in a specific direction?

Elijah was heard from again about six to ten years later when he wrote a letter from somewhere here on earth, scolding Jehoram for what he had been doing while king (2 Chron. 21:12-15).

A Double Portion of Miracles?

Here's what I thought I knew: Since Elisha asked for a double portion of Elijah's "spirit," he had exactly twice the number of miracles associated with him than Elijah did (2 Kings 2:9, 10).

Here's more to consider: Let's begin with some questions. Is keeping score of the quantity of miracles what Elisha really was asking for? Wouldn't that be a desire of the flesh? Does the Bible record every miracle these two prophets performed or were associated with? Let's remember, it is the Lord who performs the miracles. Does the Bible record every miracle Yeshua did? Does it record all the miracles the disciples and Paul were a part of? If the count of Elijah's seven miracles is affected by him not outrunning a chariot and not getting whisked off to heaven without dying a human death; wouldn't this be in conflict with the exact double number of miracles attributed to Elisha? Even the official list of Elisha's 14 miracles does not include the miracle of a dead man coming back to life after touching Elisha's bones (2 Kings 13:21). So, the count of miracles on either prophet is enough of a variable to be unable to prove this "double portion of miracles" theory.

What was Elisha really asking for? He wished to be God's representative for Israel's revival. His request was essentially "dedicated to God" because he sensed the necessity for extra spiritual empowerment for the task at hand. We have difficulty believing this account portrays his goal being to outperform Elijah and produce more miracles.

Did Elijah Die a Human Death?

Here's what I thought I knew: Elijah was taken directly to heaven and never died a human death.

Here's more to consider: To which heaven did the whirlwind take Elijah? Where the birds fly, where the planets are, or to the throne room of God? Whirlwinds do not usually extend to the latter two.

We need to set a time frame here. Joram (son of Ahab and Jezebel) reigned in the northern kingdom (Israel) for 12 years (2 Kings 3:1). We know Elijah had already been taken by the whirlwind, because they were consulting Elisha (2 Kings 3:11) when Joram (king of Israel) joined forces with Jehoshaphat; (king of Judah) to battle Moab in the last couple years of Jehoshaphat's reign (2 Kings 3:7).

After Jehoshaphat's death, Jehoram becomes the new king of Judah for an eight year reign; while Joram was still king of Israel. After Jehoram had been king for some years, Elijah sent a writing by messenger, scolding Jehoram for the improper things he had been doing while king (2 Chronicles 21:12-15). The message pronounced a judgment from God upon Jehoram, his people and his family.

This letter to Jehoram had to be approximately six to nine years after Elijah had been taken away by the whirlwind. Besides elaborating on the content of the letter, Josephus states: "For he (Elijah) was yet upon the earth" (Antiquities of the Jews 9, 5:2). Did the Lord have other work for Elijah at another location here on earth? Elijah was close enough to get word about what had taken place. He was also close enough to send a messenger with the letter of reprimand. Elijah's whirlwind experience may be similar to Philip's translation (Acts 8:39, 40).

After the letter, Jehoram suffered the last two years of his eight year reign with a bowel disease and his family was taken as predicted (2 Chron. 21:16-20); except for his youngest son Ahaziah, who reigned after Jehoram for one year. Ahaziah and Joram were both killed by Jehu, ending Joram's twelve year reign (2 Kings 9:24-29). So, the letter from Elijah was likely 7-9 years after the whirlwind, and 5-6 years into Jehoram's eight year reign.

In Harpers Bible Dictionary (page 760) numerous fasts and feasts of the Jewish calendar are listed. It states the tenth day of the second month, Ziv, was a fast to commemorate the death of Elijah. A Mid-East site is known as the tomb of Elijah. Whether it is the actual grave is anybody's guess, but they do not think of him going straight to the throne room of God without dying.

In the famous chapter of those who died in faith, Elijah must certainly be included in "the prophets" who died in faith waiting for the promise. Even though there isn't an exact list of all the prophet's names from beginning to end, Elijah ranks among the "major prophets" (Heb. 11:32). It doesn't say these all died in faith "except Elijah," does it?

Do not forget, no man has ascended up to heaven, except He that came down from heaven, Yeshua Himself (John 3:13). It is appointed unto man to die once, and after that comes judgment (Heb. 9:27). Try to find a verse that states Elijah (or Enoch) were the exceptions to the grave, good luck! In this case, the account of Elijah's death is not documented. There is also an absence of any verse in the Bible stating Elijah went straight to the throne room of God without dying.

Did Enoch Die a Human Death?

Here's what I thought I knew: Enoch was taken straight up to heaven without dying a human death (Gen. 5:24). Because of this, Enoch is one of the Two Witnesses spoken of in the book of Revelation.

Here's more to consider: There isn't much mention of Enoch in Scripture, but what it does say gives a different impression. It says Enoch walked with God for 300 years and all the days of Enoch were 365 years (Gen. 5:23). That would indicate he is not still aging and he died after 365 years. Is it possible that God took Enoch, as He later translates and buries (Deut. 34:5, 6) Moses, to a different location here on earth?

Why would Enoch be included twice (Heb. 11:5) in the famous "by faith they died" chapter, if he did not die in faith? Enoch is also implicated in the "all these who died in faith, waiting for the promise" (Heb. 11:13). If Enoch had gone straight to heaven, wouldn't he already have received that promise? No place does it say these all died "except for Enoch."

Enoch is said to have been "translated" so he would not "see" death (Heb. 11:5). Translated does not mean "to make immortal;" but "to be removed, taken away, put in another place." The Greek language has other words for dying or experiencing death. The Greek word for "see" is eidon; which means "perceive with the eyes." Was Enoch translated to another location here on earth where death could not be seen?

Was his physical life in danger at the hands of an evil society (Jude 14-16) because of his testimony of judgment? Or, was he possibly spared looking upon the death of those he cared for? Could this simply be an account telling us that because Enoch walked with God previous to Messiah's arrival; he was counted worthy to be translated spiritually into the Kingdom of redemption and forgiveness of sin? Therefore, he would not "see" the second death (John 8:51) (Col. 1:13).

There is no specific mention of Enoch being the exception to dying a human death and then standing judgment, as is appointed unto man (Heb. 9:27). Neither is there a verse identifying him as one of the Two Witnesses (Rev. 11:3).

Enoch's translation may be similar to the translation of Elijah, Moses, the boat immediately at shore (John 6:21) and Philip (Acts 8:39, 40); though Enoch's exact location and death are not recorded in Scripture. We must also keep in mind that no man has ascended to heaven except He who descended, the Lord Himself (John 3:13). Doesn't the overall teaching of Scripture indicate Enoch awaits resurrection and judgment just like everybody else that ever lived and died?

CHAPTER TWO

Tithe-The Shocking Facts!

We believe in meeting needs freely and supporting the assembly we attend. Surely the Lord honors believers who give cheerfully with money, time and resources. But, the modern day unbiblical method of threatening people with a curse from God; unless they give ten percent of their income all the time, begs to be addressed.

Here's what I thought I knew: The New Testament Church is commanded to tithe. They tell us we must donate the first ten percent of our income (the gross, not the net) to the church and we are cursed with a curse from God if we don't. It is even taught that Abram giving a tenth of the spoils of war to Melchizedek is our example to tithe money to the church today.

Here's more to consider: There is not one instruction or even a suggestion in the whole New Testament that directs us to tithe. The Old Testament does not say they ever tithed money, jewels, gold or silver. The Bible does not say they ever tithed their wages, salary or income. Since crops mature at different times, it seems they tithed food harvests from the land at the pilgrimage festivals three times a year; spring-Passover (barley), summer-Shavuot (wheat) and fall-Sukkot (fruit). Does your church only want tithes three times a year?

"First fruits" were a small token food offering and not the same thing as tithing from the full harvest. The tithe was not always the first "tenth." Sometimes, it was the last tenth or the tenth animal that passed under the rod (Lev. 27:30-32). You could not rearrange the order in which they passed. The tenth animal could be the prize of the herd, or it could be the runt.

There was a third and sixth year tithe and it also was only food (Deut. 26:12). This giving was to stay in the cities in which it was given and helped feed folks until the next harvest was

35

available (Deut. 14:28, 29). The tithes were only foods from the land and livestock. No, they were not just poor dirt farmers. Yes, they did have money. Money was not used for a tithe, because tithing was only food (Deut. 14:23).

And here is the shocker...They only gave a tenth for six years; because every seventh year the land was allowed to rest, they could only eat what grew naturally and there was no tithing every seventh year! And their food tithing system still kept everyone fed until the next crops were available (Lev. 25:21). Does your church forego tithes every seventh year?

The tithes could only be accepted by Levites, overseen by priests (descendants of Aaron). Are there many Levite priests today that can trace their lineage back to Aaron (Num. 18:21-28) without a generation gap? The tithes were only food from the land, collected in 48 designated Levitical cities, which included the six cities of refuge (Num. 35:6, 7). The Levites were to take ten percent of the tenth given (from the 48 cities) to the priests in the Jewish Temple. So, the majority of the food given, remained in the 48 cities; and only about one or two percent of the food grown actually went to the Temple to feed the priests and others there. The Temple was destroyed in 70 AD, and does not exist anymore. It was the Israelites who were told to tithe (take care of the Levites and priests) as long as they lived in the Promised Land, specifically Canaan (Deut. 12:19).

The whole tithe system was God's design to ensure everybody was fed with the abundance from the land that He gave them, for we cannot concentrate on the Lord when we are starving. The priests who served in the Temple, the Levites who taught Torah in the cities (1 Chron. 6:48, 49), the poor, widows, orphans, and even foreign travelers should not have to worry about their daily food needs or beg a meal. This was to show how wonderful Israel's God was, that nobody should go hungry; and their society, religion and loving God were far superior to pagan cultures around them. The poor were allowed to glean from the corners of others fields, and glean from harvest left on the ground (Deut. 24:19-21). The servants working in the fields were allowed to eat their fill, and even the laboring animals were not to be muzzled so they could eat while they worked (Deut. 25:4). Tithing was not a hardship for the givers, but a way to share the Lord's abundance without any hardship for the givers. They were able to sell any of the remaining 90% of their crops for money, but did not have to tithe on that increase.

They only tithed on the increase from the land. They never tithed on a harvest they did not already possess, or until they had been blessed. Poor people were not expected to tithe because they owned no land to tithe from. It was not a precise ten percent either, as the Pharisees were cutting an anise leaf so exactly. And back then, they usually would not handle money on the Sabbath. Yet today, most churches use the meeting as their money collection day.

A tithe was a tenth, but a tenth was not always a tithe. Jacob had bargained with God and did not give this tenth (not called a tithe) until God blessed him (Gen. 28:20-22). Is bargaining with God an example for us today? The Bible does not say Jacob ever gave a tenth again, or taught his children or anyone else to give a tenth. Perhaps he gave the tenth to the poor.

The Bible does not say anywhere that Abram ever tithed on his own crops, personal property or livestock. The Bible never states Abram ever had a custom of tithing to God, or that God instructed Abram to give a tenth to Melchizedek, or that he considered these spoils of war as his "own personal increase." Nor does the Bible say Abram ever instructed his children or anyone else to tithe. This was about five centuries before someone first wrote the word "tithe" in the Torah. This was also before Abram was circumcised, received the promise or his name was changed to Abraham. So, they were all basically Gentiles at this time.

The tenth Abram gave to Melchizedek was from the "spoils of war" (Heb. 7:4). The other 90% of the spoils were divided amongst the king of Sodom, Abram's men and the other kings' fighting men. Abram gave nothing from his own pocket and it was a onetime event. He could have had more of the spoils, but promised he would not take a thread of it (Gen. 14:22-24).

According to the Torah centuries later, the soldiers required one time contribution from the "spoils of war" was only (.1%), yes, that's 1/1000th (Num. 31:25-29). And according to the Torah, the peoples' contribution was only (1%), yes, that is 1/100th (Num. 31:30). If pastors try to use Abram or the Torah as the standard to teach tithing, how did they come up with 10% of our income (all the time) for our church tithing rules, from a story about a onetime portion concerning the spoils of war? By using Abram as an example and giving away 100%, were you a good steward for your family? You might need a second job, and then you can tithe on that income too!

The Assyrian culture (and others) traditionally designated a tenth of the spoils of war to the reigning king of the region, and the remainder to the victor. The king of Sodom's words support this because he considered the remaining 90% as under Abram's control, even though some of it had previously belonged to Sodom. Is this act to be taken as a command for us to tithe today? Are we to give 10% to Melchizedek and 90% to Sodom to be acceptable with God?

Remember, Melchizedek was a high priest, but he was also a king of the pagan city of Salem (Gen. 14:18). Melchizedek may very well have been attacked by the marauders also, provided some soldiers or resources for the battle, and the tenth was his rightful share. If you notice, God didn't tell Abram to give Melchizedek anything.

Was Abram making an "offering to the Lord" by giving Melchizedek a tenth of the spoils of war? After the battle and dividing of the goods took place, Abram did make an offering to the Lord, but not from the spoils of war (Gen. 15:1, 9, 10). If Abram is to be our example, should we also cut up a cow, goat and sheep for the Lord?

Melchizedek was an earthly king and appeared to honor Abrams' military leadership. Abram either honored him as the governing king of the region or his priestly office on a spiritual level. Mutual respect shows, because Melchizedek blessed Abram who had the promise (Heb. 7:6).

Unfortunately there are no recorded words from Abram to Melchizedek. Why would Melchizedek have greater status than Abram, whom God had spoken to twice (Gen. 12:1, 13:14) and appeared to one time (Gen. 12:7) already? Was Melchizedek greater because he was ending his priestly reign and Abram was just starting the fatherhood of the Jews? Melchizedek may have been one of the oldest remaining believers in Yahweh from the Noah era, who was living in a land of idolatry and was passing the spiritual torch to Abram.

I do have a question about the lesser (Abram) being blessed by the greater (Melchizedek) (Heb. 7:7). How, in the same sentence (Gen. 14:20), could Melchizedek bless Abram and then "bless" God? Was Melchizedek greater than God, because he blessed God too? Surely not! This could explain his use of "El elyon." (See "Mystery Melchizedek")

Let's take this a step further. If Abram is our example in this case, are we to join forces with the king of Sodom and Gomorrah? Remember, Abram had 318 men to join the king of Sodom and the other kings' forces. Are we to gather our own fighting men and group together with others for battle, to obtain the spoils of war to "tithe" to God? Even if Sodom, Gomorrah and the other kings provided an equal number of men, that was a formidable force. It had previously been four bad kings against five (Gen. 14:9).

Abram's battle caused mass bloodshed, (Hebrews 7:1 calls it a slaughter) because they took everything the other people had, as well as the remaining people for slaves. Josephus stated some were slain while they slept in their beds and others were so drunk they could not fight and ran. He also indicates Melchizedek was hospitable and supplied all the men with provisions for feasting in abundance (Antiquities of the Jews, book one; 10:1, 2). Is this killing and pillaging to be our example to obtain tithes for the Lord? Are the spoils of war and slaves offered as "tithes" something the Lord would consider acceptable? Remember, tithes were always foods from the land for the Levites, priests, poor, etc. as described in all the other Bible verses about tithing.

The king of Sodom was more interested in the people (prisoners of war?) than the goods, though some of the goods had previously belonged to Sodom (Gen. 14:21). If Abram gave Melchizedek a tenth of "all," that would mean a tenth of the conquered slaves also. Are slaves a Godly contribution? Was the act of Abram (after a slaughter) giving Melchizedek (the church?) a tenth of the spoils of war, something we should make into church doctrine today? How much of this ancient account of slaughter, looting and capturing of slaves is an example for us today?

Should honest Bible students create a false tithe lesson from half a verse in Genesis, while blindly ignoring the rest of the verses? Can't we give freely now without creating and perpetuating this error about back then?

Never are Gentiles instructed to tithe in the New Testament. The early church never tithed. They met needs by giving freely when needs arose. This is what free-will offering is all about. Tithing does not mean you owe ten percent of your income from every paycheck. It always referred to food for the Levites, priests, widows, poor, etc.

Did Paul or Yeshua ever tithe or collect tithes? There was still a Jewish Temple with Levites and priests in their day and the tithing of foods was still in effect. Yeshua did not even pay the Temple tax (law #404, Exod. 30:13-16) out of His own pocket, or from the treasury Judas held. Yeshua sent him to catch a fish and use the coin from the fish's mouth to pay the tax, so they wouldn't be offended. Did you notice He only paid for Himself and Peter (Matt. 17:24-27), not the other eleven? Anyway, why should He have to pay a tax to the Lord of the Temple? He "was" the Lord of the Temple!

Fishermen did not tithe of their fish. Tithe was only food from the land. Carpenters did not tithe; the wagon makers (that hauled the crops) did not tithe; the basket weavers (that held the crops) did not tithe; the servants picking the crops did not tithe; cobblers did not tithe; potters did not tithe; garment makers did not tithe; tent makers did not tithe; prostitutes did not tithe; jewelers did not tithe, etc. Only farmers and owners of livestock tithed from the increase of the land.

Why is tithing one of the only things out of the Torah that modern clergy seem to want to keep in effect? It works so effectively to convince you to part with your money, that's why.

If we are going to extract convenient bits and pieces from the Torah, are we going to start sacrificing sheep again? What about the people commanding us to tithe, are they eating kosher food according to the Torah? Or is that a part of the Law we don't have to regard anymore? Are we to bring back stoning naughty people too? Are we going back to the shadow after we have the Light?

The only time money was involved (I told you they had money) was when there was too much food to transport or it was too far to transport it. Then it should be sold locally, and after travel and upon arrival, the money should buy whatever food and drink you liked (Deut. 14:22-28). Then, you would sit down to eat, drink and share before the Lord. Still, no money was ever tithed. It must have been like a great big potluck dinner with folks feasting together and rejoicing before the Lord.

There was also a provision for you to "buy back" your tithe. The priest would put a fair value to whatever you wished to buy back and then add one fifth the value (20%). Then you could (with money) purchase back something you wished to keep that you had previously tithed (Num. 27:12-13, 19, 27, 30-31).

They always had the Temple treasury to collect money offerings as people were led to give. It was never a mandatory ten percent. This is what Yeshua was watching when the widow gave two mites and it was a greater gift than other's larger donations (Mark 12:41-44) (Luke 21:1-4).

The verses in Hebrews Chapter 7 merely state Abram gave a tenth of the spoils of battle and that the Levites and priests did accept tithes. The verses in Hebrews Chapter 7 do not instruct or even suggest that anybody should tithe.

41

The Lord criticized the Pharisees for being so careful to cut up an anise leaf (still only food). Their error was ignoring the needs of those around them by not showing the love, forgiveness and mercy that the Lord prefers (Matt. 23:23).

Here are the verses so often misapplied to support "money" as tithing: "Will a man rob God? Yet ye have robbed me. But ye say wherein have we robbed thee? In tithes and offerings, ye are cursed with a curse for ye have robbed me, even this whole nation. Bring ye all the tithes into the store house, that there may be "meat" (food) in mine house, test me on this says the Lord of hosts" (Malachi 3:8-10). Then, you'll notice, they stop reading.

We cannot take just one verse (completely out of context) to support a tithe doctrine without reading the rest of the story. Nearly all of the first three chapters of Malachi are scolding the Levites and the priests about impure offerings and faulty sacrifices of crops and livestock (Mal. 1:6; 2:1, 7, 8, 13). This reprimand of the priests continues through Chapter Three. Notice (Mal. 1:6, 7, 12, 13; 2:17; 3:7, 8, 13) how many times the priests keep asking, "How have we been doing this?" Then the Lord answers them. The priests were even cheating widows, orphans and workers of their "pay"(Mal. 3:5).

Israel still had the Temple, they still had Levites and priests, and they were still giving food in "quantity" so there would be meat in the Lord's house. The Lord was upset with the "quality" of the giving and the improper priestly activity. The Lord even asks if their human governor would accept these defective offerings (Mal. 1:8). Yet, in actuality, they were trying to offer them to the Creator of all.

Their hearts weren't right in their priestly office. Therefore, it could only have been the priests (even the whole nation or tribe of Levites) who were robbing God with impure offerings and inferior foods in the Temple, because the regular people did not perform these duties. Surely it did not take long for the people to follow the priest's example of laziness and indifference. The Lord considered it polluted (Mal. 1:12). In

Nehemiah's day, the giving had stopped and the Levites had to go back to farming to support their own families (Neh. 13:10).

What was the curse that could happen if they did not improve their spirit of giving with the offerings and tithes of foods from the land? With proper giving, the Lord indicates the fruit of their soil would not be devoured and their vines wouldn't drop their fruit early giving bountiful harvest (Mal. 3:10-12). There remains the understanding that tithe was only foods from the land and livestock. The curse was associated with the blessing of, or the negative effect on their crops. This is not so much of a curse, but more the threat of a curse upon their food source. Aren't you relieved to find out this curse is not directed at you?

Let's keep this in context. Malachi is a Jewish prophet about 500 years before Messiah. He is mainly speaking to the Levites and priests concerning the inferior "food" offerings and "animal" sacrifices in the Jewish Temple. Only the priests gave offerings in the Temple; that was not the task of a normal worshiper. Malachi was not speaking to Gentiles, some 2,500 years later, about sending ten percent of their income to some TV shyster! Remember, it was Israel who was instructed to tithe food for the Levites and priests, as long as they occupied and lived in the Promised Land (Deut.12:19).

The Catholic Church was the first to start extracting money as tithes, somewhere between 585 A.D. and the 8th or 9th centuries, to better fund their church. They found that instead of only produce and livestock, from only farmers three times every year, they could get cash from everybody, all the time! This method of tithing is totally unbiblical. Do you see what this has turned into today? The Catholic Church has been collecting ill-gotten gain for over 1,200 years now, is the richest institution on earth and does more worldwide fiscal business each year than the United States.

Christian tithing is absent in Scripture. The only thing similar between Torah food tithing and tricking Christians to tithe their money; is the word "tenth." There is not one person in the Bible who ever tithed in the manner that many Christians are instructed to today. We should not be as the majority who peddle the Word of God (2 Cor. 2:17).

Do you mean to tell me that after years of Bible College, seminary and years of Bible study, these preachers conveniently never found any information that biblical tithing was only foods from the land? I am over 50 years old, and I have yet to hear any of this voiced from a pulpit. It's one thing, if a preacher did not know this and changes as soon as he finds out. But, it is quite another, if he did know and continued to perpetuate the deceit. Would that mean the preacher did not have enough faith in the Lord or his congregation to give freely, so as to cover all the needs of the church? Or, would it mean the preacher wanted more money?

The finest TV pulpiteers money can buy tell us that God owns everything and He does not need your money. Then, in the next breath they tell us we are cursed with a curse from God if we don't send them our tithe money. Are they Levites or priests? Are they in 48 cities or the Jewish Temple storehouse? Do they want every tenth tomato out of your garden once a year? No, they want your hard-earned cash from every paycheck. They never ask you to send food from the land such as beets, apples, carrots, squash, beans, onions, a lamb or a calf as a donation, do they?

Not only will brother and sister super Christian ask for ten percent of the gross (not the net); but they will ask for extra offerings above and beyond this tithing scam. Is giving a set amount of 10 % an exact formula to "guarantee" your financial success? If you want more money (blessings), do you mechanically and systematically give above and beyond this meager ten percent starting point to attain mega-riches? This is the fleecing of the Christian community disguised as "Godly giving," while people are actually giving out of a pure heart.

Some of these TV ministries are taking in more than $50 or $100 million dollars a year, each! Are you sickened at these week long beg-a-thons on the Christian circus networks? Are you grieved by the polished Hollywood infomercial, drive-thru

Christianity presented by the big money mega churches? Are you appalled at the sophisticated snake oil sermons that these TV charlatans designed to, steal widow's pensions, rob poor folks on a fixed income, pilfer welfare recipient's money, working family's wages, single parent's income, and old people's social security checks? Aren't these the folks the church is supposed to be taking care of in the first place? Aren't they who the food tithe was partly for originally?

To give 10 % from an income of $200,000; leaves $180,000 to live on. But, for someone who only makes $12,000 a year; to give 10% would take food off the table, cancel insurance, delay a heat or light bill, delay a doctor or dental visit and create a condition of financial distress; making even auto maintenance an unknown luxury! God never intended your giving to be a burden for your family or compromise your living conditions.

Did you notice the begging always comes with a pitch that you will be blessed with a 30, 60 or 100 fold increase for doing so; thus promoting an expectant "greed" in the giver? Look at the verses they use to verify this (Matt. 13:8, 23) (Mark 4:8, 20). The Lord is actually telling and explaining a parable about us producing fruit for Him; and not about filling your pockets or bank account. Anyway, if the gift of salvation is free, they neglected to inform us that we will now owe an offering plate ten percent of our money for the rest of our lives! Is salvation really a free gift, if you have to work continuously to pay for it?

Hey, I know, send me an unstoppable favor harvest seed of $10,000, or just 4 easy payments of $2,500 each on your Visa card; and I will teach you how to be prosperous and stay out of debt.

Mystery Melchizedek

Here is some interesting information you can find about a mysterious Bible character. Some folks say Melchizedek was Shem, the son of Noah. This doesn't hold up because Shem has known lineage. Some folks say Melchizedek was a secret visit from the Lord. This view has little basis or merit.

Some folks think Melchizedek was just a pagan priest and king of a pagan city called Salem. He was also in some form of alliance with the kings of Sodom and Gomorrah located close by. This view has an interesting aspect. We must keep in mind; pagan did not mean they were atheists who didn't believe in God. Pagans usually believed in many gods.

When Melchizedek said, "God most high," he used the words "El elyon" (Gen. 14:20). This was a common term at the time for Baal, and was not (in record) used for YHVH before or after this, until about 1,000 yrs. later. Two verses later when Abram said, he promised "God most high" he would not take any of the spoils; he used the name "YHVH" (Gen. 14:22).

Was Melchizedek giving credit to Baal for Abram's success in battle? El elyon was a commonly used for Baal and/or his father. Baal (in pagan worship) was also called the maker of heaven and earth. Half of his name Zedek was associated with Jupiter and a pagan god of justice in the Assyrian/Phoenician culture. Salem (Shalim) was their god of the dusk.

If Abram became the first Hebrew, then everyone else was kind of a Gentile, huh? Even if they were to have believed in the God of Adam and Noah, there were no actual Hebrews yet. Salem was a pagan city under pagan influence and rule until centuries later, when it became Jerusalem.

Abram gave Melchizedek a tenth of the spoils of war, but it was not produce from the land as in the Torah about 500 years later. If the Torah as our standard, it dictated 1/1000th was the requirement of the spoils of war, one time and not weekly (Num. 31:25-30). Just after Abram gave a tenth to Melchizedek; he did make an offering to God (Gen. 15:1-10), but not from the spoils! Had the tenth of war spoils really been for the Lord?

So, what about Hebrews Chapter Seven? First of all, let us realize there is not a verse that instructs or even suggests
46

anyone should tithe in the whole chapter. The word tenth (or in some Bibles, tithe) was translated from the same Greek word. The word in (Heb. 7:5) is a bit different in respect to the Levite priests, who collected food tithes from the people, but this is not the focus of the context.

The writer to the Hebrews used their respect for Abraham to show how the priesthood of Yeshua was similar to, but greater than the king/priesthood of Melchizedek. If the Melchizedek king/priesthood was considered greater than Abraham (with the lineage of the Levitical priesthood in his loins); then the order of Yeshua's King/Priesthood is greater than all.

The writer of Hebrews uses Melchizedek being priest and king to establish and prove Yeshua's King/Priesthood was similar to, but greater than; because it also did not come through Levitical lineage, but by divine appointment. The Jews recorded their ancestry, but not those from other cultures; which, as with YHVH, no beginning or ending is recorded for Melchizedek.

Side Note: Since Methuselah was alive for a couple hundred years before Adam died, and he was alive until the flood; Methuselah would have shared stories about Adam and Eve with his grandson Noah and Noah's sons also. It stands to reason Abraham and Melchizedek both could have gotten oral stories right from Adam thru just one or two ear witnesses.

Taking that into account, I feel more comfortable with the idea Melchizedek was possibly one of the oldest living believers from the Noah era, who ended up being a king and priest of a pagan city. He still believed in the True God of Adam and Noah, while in a pagan environment. But wouldn't you think he had to put up with some degree of pollution of pagan worship in the city or culture, or from surrounding pagan cities like Sodom and Gomorrah? This was even before Abram became the father of the Jews, so he was also a Gentile at the time, huh?

What if Melchizedek was paying homage to Baal (El-elyon) in (Gen. 14:20); and the tenth was the custom of the region to the reigning king? With this in mind, it doesn't seem to affect what took place in (Gen. 14) or the comparison made to his king/priesthood in Hebrews Chapter Seven. It makes no difference if Melchizedek believed in Baal and was mistakenly honored over time; or he believed in Baal yet recognized the power of the God of Abram; or he believed in YHVH, but used a different name for Him. The point to the Hebrews doesn't seem to hinge on any of these factors. The main focus is the Kingship and Priesthood of Messiah surpasses all.

Does the Law of Moses Apply to us Today?

Here's what I thought I knew: The Law of Moses is outdated and over, it was nailed to the cross and does not apply to New Testament believers today. We are now under Grace.

Here's more to consider: The Torah, before and after Messiah, is a teaching/instruction manual or mirror reflecting what He desires from us. Sin is transgression of God's teaching and carries the meaning of "falling short, missing the mark." Even now, under grace, the Torah is still God's instructions given to guide us in a life more abundant in love, hope, faith and joy to share with others. The Torah is a measure of personal and internal progress as we follow His paths directing us to our Messiah. To eliminate the Torah from the New Testament and our lives would be unbiblical as well as catastrophic. Without the Torah, how would any of us know who the true Messiah is?

Yeshua said specifically that He did not come to destroy the Torah, and not one jot or tittle will pass away (Matt. 5:17-20). Messiah not only endorsed the Torah and commandments, but added the spiritual aspect to give it deeper meaning. We should exceed the righteousness of the Pharisees. More is expected from us, outward and inward, than the chief priests were accomplishing. Then He explains it in detail for about three chapters. Did you notice, whenever Yeshua quoted Scripture, it was from the Torah, or the Old Testament? It was the same with Paul. The New Testament is very clear; we should have the Torah written upon our hearts, and not just display it outwardly (Heb. 8:10). Is the wisdom from the verse in (Proverbs 28:9) obsolete now too? What about (Jer. 31:33)?

When the Bereans searched the Scriptures daily, they did not have any of the New Testament to search (Acts 17:11). They were talking about the Torah and the Tanakh (the Old Testament). Paul was advocating the Torah when saying, all Scripture is given for instruction, reproof, etc. There was no New Testament at that time; he was referring to the Torah. The principle of the Torah hinges on the two points of how to honor God and live with your fellow man, but not to the exclusion of the other points of the Torah (Mark 12:29-31). Even on Judgment Day the Lord said He would reject those who practice "lawlessness" (Matt. 7:23), which means Torah-lessness.

Many of our laws today stem from the Torah of Moses, even including the intent to commit. If the Torah is over, what do we base our salvation on? The very premise and promise of the blood covering for sin is based in the Torah (Lev. 17:11). If the Torah is now null and void, then the blood shed to atone for our sin is now invalid too. Surely this is not the case. If the Torah is over, how do we know what sin is? If the Torah is over, why do so many refer to it for proof texts and teaching? Though the sacrificial system is complete in Messiah, we still have God's instruction book on how to live with each other and for Him. It was always a focus inward, not on the outward ritual.

How can we take the Jewish religion, disregard the Torah (which is now called the Law of Moses) and call it our own new Christian religion? When was the last time you did not wash before eating, killed someone, stole or committed adultery? Have you eaten an animal lately that you found dead, and did not know how it died? You are probably following much of the Torah without realizing it, and not giving God the credit.

The Torah (Rom. 3:20) teaches us what sin is and our need for grace. Salvation comes by faith in who Messiah is and what He did. The Torah isn't how we are saved, but guidance on how we should strive to live and love because we "are" saved, right?

49

Should Women Only Wear Dresses?

Here's what I thought I knew: Women should wear dresses exclusively. Because wearing slacks of any type would be wearing man's clothes and not just be a sin, but an abomination.

Here is the verse in question: A woman shall not wear that which pertains to a man and a man shall not wear that which pertains to a woman; whoever does these things is an abomination to the Lord your God (Deut. 22:5).

Here's more to consider: This verse is not talking about cross dressing or transvestites. At the time this was written, even the men wore skirts! Look up these verses mentioning skirts in your Bible (Deut. 22:30) (Ruth 3:9) (Hag. 2:12) (Zech. 8:23). Pants or trousers had not been invented yet.

The word "man" in (Deut. 22:5) is not the normal Hebrew word for man. It is the word "geber," for "soldier or mighty man." The verse should read, "A woman shall not wear that which pertains to a soldier, and a soldier shall not wear that which pertains to a woman."

Adam Clarke noted that Canaanite women were accustomed to exchanging clothes with their soldiers, to appear in armor when praying to Venus/Astarte/Ashtaroth for victory in battle. The command in the Torah was simply telling the Israelites not to do as the pagans do. Josephus makes a specific reference to this in his account (Antiquities of the Jews, book 4, 8:43). He said, "Take care, especially in your battles, that no woman uses the habit of a man, nor man the garment of a woman."

If women have to follow this rule in (Deut. 22:5), shouldn't we all have to follow all the verses surrounding it? Can we just pick and choose any verses out of the Torah we want to enforce? Here are a few verses from the same chapter to consider:

Do we have to make a battlement (railing) (Deut. 22:8) for the roof of a new house? Though a good idea not to, do we sin by mixing seeds (Deut. 22:9) in our vineyards?

Do we avoid garments (Deut. 22:11) with two different fabrics? Do we have to put fringes (Deut. 22:12) on the four corners of our vesture anymore?

Do we still stone (Deut. 22:13-21) non-virgins? Are we going to exclude any man from the congregation (Deut. 23:1) because he had a groin injury?

Are we to exclude a poor illegitimate orphan (Deut. 23:2) from the congregation? Are we going to start sacrificing sheep again? Isn't it interesting, this one verse really only affects and suppresses women? Doesn't His Grace now allow us to dress in modesty, especially if we are not conflicting with the Torah? Are the men actually eating kosher food according to the same Torah, from which they are requiring their women follow this other rule?

How modest is it, if a woman in a dress jumps on a trampoline, goes skydiving or skiing? How comfortable is it, if she rides a trail bike or horse, plays softball or goes rock climbing while wearing a dress? Are women to be excluded from numerous activities because wearing pants would be a sin?

Kosher Food

Here's what I thought I knew: There is no direct command to change eating habits given in the New Testament, so the Torah/Law of Moses is still valid and in effect. We must still avoid pork, shellfish and other previously prohibited foods.

Here's more to consider: The abstaining from certain foods was a part of the Torah (Law of Moses). Is eating kosher still mandatory, or is it just fitting and proper to now follow the wisdom God has already established? You would be considered ceremonially unclean if you were to eat something improper, touch a dead person or animal, have marital relations, deliver a child, be a leper or have a running sore. The corrective measure for these infractions was washing and waiting for sundown. Some infractions required a sacrifice also. Unclean did not mean abomination, it meant impure. Why would their eating habits be grouped with these other seeming unrelated activities, like child birth?

Let's think about this. If one man took a bite of pork one hour before sundown, then washed, in one hour he would be considered clean again. Another man took a bite of pork one hour after sundown, washed right away, but had to wait until sundown the following day to be considered clean again.

Are we under the sin penalty of the Torah anymore? Are we going back to the shadow after we found the Light? Are we going to sacrifice sheep again? Let's remember, eating kosher is not only avoiding certain foods; it also includes how the food is handled, stored, prepared and even the clean up afterwards. It is nearly impossible to keep perfectly kosher today.

The Israelites were instructed not to eat fat (Lev. 7:23). They could not touch a dead animal, (Lev. 11:8, 39) but they could use the fat for any other purpose, as long as they did not eat it (Lev. 7:24). How did they use the fat of a dead animal without touching it? They would become unclean by eating an animal that dies of itself, (Lev. 11:39, 40) yet they could sell that animal to a stranger (Deut. 14:21). If these things were sins against God, would these laws be so broad and flexible? Remember, all foods had been acceptable (minus the blood) before the Exodus into the wilderness (Gen. 9:1-4).

The animals that Noah took on the ark were seven pair of clean animals, seven pair of birds of the air and one pair of animals that are "not clean" (Gen. 7:2, 3). The term "not clean" has nothing to do with the unclean food laws in the Torah. The Torah had not been written yet. The term "not clean" referred to "not acceptable for sacrifice."

When Noah came off of the ark, God gave man every moving

thing that lives for food, except the blood (Gen. 9:3, 4). So it was only for a period of time, from the wilderness to Messiah, that the food rule of Moses was a command. Now, it is just a good decision on our part to follow the teaching in the Torah.

The New Testament is very clear, even adamant, that we are not under the penalty of the Torah anymore. And if you adhere to one point of the Law, you are responsible to carry out every letter of the impossible Law (Gal. 3:10).

Paul did not think it mattered if you eat only vegetables or meat too. Nobody should judge you for what you eat. Neither should you judge anyone for what meat they eat (Romans 14:2-4). Paul said to not let anyone judge you in meat or drink (Col. 2:16).

Paul states to the Romans, that all things are indeed clean (Romans 14:20, 21). Paul was "persuaded by the Lord that there is nothing unclean of itself" (Romans 14:13-17). If your decision is based on your faith for God, it seems either eating habit is acceptable (Rom. 14:22, 23). If you are not eating kosher, yet wondering if it is okay, then you are wrong. If you are eating kosher, wondering if you really have to, or are sure you are better than others, wrong again. Whatever we are eating or not eating should honor the Lord and not be causing an issue or division between us and someone else, or with God.

Believers were instructed to watch for four things: abstain from what has been sacrificed to idols, abstain from blood, abstain from what is strangled and avoid any form of sexual immorality (Acts 15:29). Did you notice three of these four instructions (all originating from the Torah) are food oriented?

Paul surely would have eaten kosher if left to his choice, or if he was in the company of Jews. But, if he became as Greeks or Romans so as to save some; do you think he would have made a big fuss over a dish of food (1 Cor. 9:19-23) when souls to be saved were at stake? As long as the blood was drained, it wasn't strangled or wasn't offered to idols, (1 Cor. 10: 23-33) didn't Paul consider it lawful? Now, because it does not create an "unclean" condition; we can eat with others without

53

offending them away from Messiah over some food on the table.

Yeshua said what goes in the mouth and comes out of the body does not defile a man, thus cleansing "all" foods (Mark 7:19). Every creature of God is good, and nothing to be refused if it be received with thanksgiving (1 Tim. 4:4).

What does this all boil down to? We can now have the freedom to eat anything, yet we can still freely choose not to eat certain things (1 Cor. 6:12-20). Rather than our glumly and religiously following an eating rule, is the Lord simply looking for our happy attitude and willing decision to eat as kosher as possible? Try abstaining from pork for a month or two and then pig out! Pay particular attention to how your body feels and functions for the next couple days after consuming the pork. You might be surprised.

Reports show how the toxins are stored in the fat of pork. Shellfish are nothing more than living filters and lobsters are just big tasty underwater cockroaches. Even if it is okay to eat these things, it surely is not beneficial and is healthier for us not to consume these foods. They were put there to filter and clean the water and earth. We've been industrially harvesting the scavengers and filters so heavily that limits on the seasons have to be enforced. Is the increasing world pollution happening because we are harvesting and eating the scavengers and filtering agents by the millions of tons every year? Do you eat the filter when you clean your aquarium?

Eating scavengers can only be to the long term detriment of our health and the proper function of the earth's eco-system. Aren't there enough varieties of good food to eat without consuming the scavengers and filters? Aren't we supposed to be wise stewards of the earth and our bodies?

Our Creator has already given us the instruction manual (Torah). We may not be under the penalty of the Law or "required" to eat kosher for salvation; but shouldn't our eating choices reflect the teaching, insight and understanding that God has already written in His Word?

Peter's Rooftop Vision

Here's what I thought I knew: Peter's rooftop vision of the sheet covered with unclean animals descending from above marks the point in time when God began to allow the eating of pork, shellfish and other previously prohibited foods (Acts 10:10-16).

Here's more to consider: For Peter was told, "Rise, Peter; kill and eat and call not thou common." While Peter wondered what this vision should mean, the men from Cornelius' house came knocking on the door (Acts10:17). Then, the Ruach told Peter to go with them, for they had been sent by Him. When Peter arrived at Cornelius' house, he obviously understood the vision, because he said; "God hath showed me that I should not call any "man" common or unclean" (Acts 10:28). This was the first time the gospel had been shared with Gentiles, for it had only been delivered to Israel up to this time.

There is not even a suggestion to make any change in eating habits in the whole chapter. This would likely be the 3 1/2 year mark since the Lord was crucified. This would also be the point in time when the 490 years, appointed upon Israel and Jerusalem, was completed (Dan. 9:24-27). The vision was a sign to Peter that Israel's exclusivity to God was over and salvation was now available to all peoples, nations and tongues. If this had been a command about changing kosher eating habits, should Peter have risen, killed and eaten the Gentiles?

Is Sunday really the New Sabbath?

Here's what I thought I knew: The Sabbath was changed from Saturday to Sunday because His resurrection was on the first day of the week. Therefore, we should go to church on the day of the week that He rose from the dead.

Here's more to consider: There is not one verse in the Bible that says the Sabbath changed to any other day. Ask any Jewish person politely what day the Sabbath is. The Saturday Sabbath has been observed farther back than 1,000 BC.

Yeshua observed the Sabbath by reading in the synagogue (Mark 1:21) (Mark 8:2) (Luke 4:16) (Luke 13:10). Yeshua taught at Capernaum on the Sabbath (Luke 4:31). Yeshua said the Sabbath was made for man, and He is the Lord of the Sabbath (Mark 2:27, 28).

Everybody still observed the Sabbath when Yeshua was in the tomb (Mark 16:1) (Luke 23:56). Paul observed the Sabbath in the synagogue at Thessalonica. For three Sabbaths he reasoned with them from the Scriptures (Acts 17:1-3). Paul went to Antioch and was asked to speak in the synagogue for the Sabbath service (Acts 13:14, 15). The whole city gathered to hear Paul speak the Word of the Lord on the "next" Sabbath (Acts 13:44).

Moses is preached in synagogues in every city on the Sabbath from the earliest times (Acts 15:21). The people were silent as they heard Paul and Barnabas speak about the New Covenant (Acts 15:12). Paul reasoned with both Jews and Greeks in the synagogues every Sabbath (Acts 18:4). He spoke of things that astonished and amazed, and even angered listeners.

Paul and his group spoke to women gathered at a place of prayer on the Sabbath (Acts 16:13). The New Testament church not only observed the Saturday Sabbath, but it seems they would meet in or out of the Temple on just about any day of the week.

There is no indication in the Bible that the Sabbath has changed to a different day. It has not been God, but men who have changed the Sabbath to Sunday. The following are a few official statements from leaders of different denominations about the Sabbath.

Baptist: There is nothing in Scripture that requires us to keep Sunday rather than Saturday as a holy day (Harold Lindsell, former editor of "Christianity Today"-Nov. 5, 1976).

Episcopal: The Bible commandment says on the seventh day thou shalt rest. That is Saturday. Nowhere in the Bible is it laid down that worship should be done on Sunday (Philip Carrington, Toronto Daily Star, Oct. 26, 1949).

Methodist: The reason we observe the first day instead of the seventh is based on no positive command. One will search the Scriptures in vain for authority to change from the seventh day to the first (Clovis G. Chappell, Ten Rules for Living, page 61).

Catholic: Sunday is a Catholic institution, and its claims to observation can be defended only on Catholic principles. From beginning to end of Scripture, there is not a single passage that warrants the transfer of weekly public worship from the last day of the week to the first (Catholic Press).

If this is common knowledge, why is everybody still going to church on Sunday? The Orthodox Jews still observe the Sabbath on Saturday. The Messianic Jews still observe the Sabbath on Saturday.

How did this change from Saturday to Sunday come about? It was the Roman Catholic Church who changed worship from Saturday to Sunday at the Council of Laodicea (The Convert's Catechism of Catholic Doctrine, 3rd Edition, page 50).

And the act is a "mark" of her ecclesiastical power and authority in religious matters (H.F. Thomas, Chancellor of Cardinal Gibbons). Isn't it interesting, this change is referred to as a "mark" of the papacy's authority?

This reminds me of a verse about a leader who speaks against the Most High and who has the desire to change "times and laws" (Dan. 7:25). Rome has persecuted and tried to eliminate Judaism for centuries. Is this Sabbath change just one more fulfillment of Daniel's prophecy, which was also revealed by John (Rev. 17:9), from the big church in Rome? Should we be observing the Sunday worship that has been changed by Catholicism? Or should we be worshiping on the Saturday Sabbath that God instituted? YHVH thought the Sabbath was

57

important enough to make a commandment to remember to observe it (Exod. 20:8-11). God said the Sabbath would be a sign (Exod. 31:12-17) for all generations that He is the Lord.

Yeshua expected the Sabbath would be observed years in the future when predicting they would pray their travel would not be in winter or on a Sabbath (Matt. 24:20). It is the ones who keep His commandments and testify of Messiah that the dragon makes war with (Rev. 12:17). The saints are the ones who keep the commandments of God (Rev. 14:12). Isn't observing the Sabbath one of the commandments?

Some people attempt to rationalize a change from Saturday to Sunday as the new Sabbath by using (Acts 20:7). Because of the group gathering together to break bread on the first day of the week, it is erroneously assumed that Paul approved of changing Sunday into the new Sabbath. Besides this account sounding like a Sabbath service that simply ran over and extended late into the night; where is any specific or even a vague mention of any change in the Sabbath day? How did they know it was the first day of the week? Because the Sabbath day had just ended!

And notice, Paul did not leave to travel on the Sabbath that had just ended, but waited until the next day (the first day of the week) to depart. To think that Paul, a Torah quoting Jew, would take it upon himself to alter or change the long established Jewish Sabbath; is utterly without foundation. And we cannot think Paul had abandoned his Jewish faith, because it says he had just finished observing the feast of Unleavened Bread a few days before he arrived at Troas (Acts 20:6).

Draw your own conclusions, but if the last verses in Isaiah refer to our future, we might expect a Sabbath to observe in the new heavens and new earth (Isa. 66:22-24); and you can bet it won't be Sunday!

CHAPTER THREE

What is in a Name?

In English we call him Jesus Christ. This is a translation from Hebrew and Greek through Latin into English. In Latin or Spanish, Jesus Christ is pronounced "hay zeus kris tos," and it is still a translation of Yeshua the Messiah. "Yeshua ha Mashiach" is how you would have said "Jesus the Messiah" 2,000 years ago. This is what they called Him face to face back then, and isn't this what He should still be called today? If God does not change, why should we change His name through translations? Messiah stands for the Jewish God revealed in human form, making a long awaited, prophesied visit to His people.

Why would we call the Lord God of the universe by a translated name? My name is Peter, but I do not wish to be called Pedro. A British lady used to pronounce my name "Peet-ah." (I kind of liked that) But, pronunciation is secondary in importance to the authority of the identity represented by the name. The Bible is very clear that there is power and authority in the identity and name of Yeshua; given for our Creator, Lord, Saviour and King.

Why should His name be translated through other languages into English here in our day? We go out of our way to pronounce all the other Bible names correctly. Isn't it more important to do the same for God's name? In Hebrew, God's name is actually more of a verb than a noun; meaning unfinished, continuous action.

The Hebrew language has no letter with the "J" sound. So, the English version and use of Jesus and Jehovah are not being pronounced as they would be in the original language, which would be Yeshua and Yahveh. The Tetragrammaton is YHVH, and in Hebrew the symbolism for it when written is: Yod (open hand) Hey (behold) Vav (nail) Hey (behold).

Even a title is important. The Jewish priests wanted Pilate to change the sign on the cross because it announced Yeshua of

Nazareth as the King of the Jews (John 19:19-22). They had rejected His claim of being their Messiah. The priests had just gotten the Lord crucified for claiming to be YHVH, and they were now upset because the sign above Him plainly declared He was their King!

Could we be missing out on some of the power in His name by using the same translated name of "Jesus" as LDS, JW's, Protestantism and Rome? Not only is God's name mispronounced, but these groups all have a different definition of God's identity and cannot agree or function as one body.

When you meet someone, isn't it important to learn their name and pronounce it properly? Didn't they use "Adonai" so they wouldn't accidently miss-pronounce God's name? All the more, shouldn't we now try to pronounce the Lord's name correctly?

Are you aware that the word "Yeshua" was used over 100 times in the Old Testament? Look up "salvation" in your concordance. It is translated from the Hebrew word "Yeshua." Even Yeshua's very name means "YHVH Saviour, salvation, God saves" (Ps. 118:14). Therefore, Yeshua the Messiah is the One Lord in human form, the Saviour, the Shepherd, the mighty God, and everlasting Father (Isa. 9:6).

Yeshua is now the only name given for our Saviour and King. To honor the Lord of the Bible, I will use Yeshua instead of "Jesus."

Laid in a Manger

Here's what I thought I knew: The "manger" where Messiah was born resembled a barn-like structure; in which travelers kept their animals while they stayed at an inn.

Here's more to consider: The original word that manger was translated from means "food box or feeding trough." She wrapped Him in swaddling clothes and laid Him in a manger (Luke 2:7). Mary had most likely lined a food trough with hay or some sort of padding, wrapped Him in swaddling clothes and used the feed box for a temporary crib. Even the shepherds had been instructed by the angels, to look for a baby in swaddling clothes in a food trough (Luke 2:12).

Joseph and Mary had to travel about 70 miles from Nazareth to his hometown Bethlehem per decree. There is a chance there were still relatives living in Bethlehem that Joseph, Mary and other relations could have stayed with while there. The word kataluma (inn) means "guest chamber," which was the front room, common in private residences to receive guests. Guest chamber would equal the parlor or living room today. This is not the same word for "inn" (pando) where the Good Samaritan found hospitable accommodations at a "receiving house" for hire (Luke 10:34). Hotels were not that common back then and nobody would have likely stayed in Bethlehem, with the big city of Jerusalem so close by. If other relatives were visiting Bethlehem also, there may not have been much room in the guest chamber (kataluma) to lay the baby. So, they may have used the protective room/shelter for the flocks during inclement weather, where a feed trough or grain box would have been a common fixture. But, they still may have been staying with relatives, a forced family reunion of sorts.

Another thing to research is Migdal Eder. If they were in northern Bethlehem and it was the fall Sukkot observance, they would have traditionally stayed in tents to remember the wilderness. There was also the Temple Tower to oversee and protect the flocks from robbers and predators. The shepherds may even have been Rabbinical Shepherds, who would oversee the birthing tents or caves, and would select the unblemished lambs.

Since the priest's garments would be bloody from all the sacrificing, they would wash them and cut them into strips, and these would be the "swaddling clothes" used to wrap the lambs, protecting them from blemish. If they were in a "barn" type atmosphere when Messiah was born, it is likely that only lambs would have been there and no other assorted animals (with a food box likely nearby). What if Messiah was either born; or circumcised and named on the eight day of Sukkot, which is the celebration of the Water and the Word.

Side Note: Bethlehem means "house of bread." That would symbolize the Bread of life was born in the house of Bread and laid in a box which held grain; which is the basic and principle ingredient for bread (John 6:48, 51).

Naming the baby and circumcision may have been a private affair and they did not have to take the baby into the Temple on the eighth day for circumcision (Luke 2:21). If so, Jerusalem was only a couple miles away from Bethlehem. Did they stay in Bethlehem for a week or so, go to the Temple on the eighth day and then leave for the 70 mile trip back to Nazareth?

But wait, Mary would have to be in Jerusalem for the Temple purification ritual, 40 days after childbirth (Lev.12:2-8). Did they just stay in Bethlehem for another month or so, and avoid a second 140 mile round trip? After childbirth, would they have made a grueling trip back to Nazareth with a newborn, only to make the same journey for a second time, a short while later? Unfortunately the details of their stay and a second trip are not provided. It just tells us of one trip to Bethlehem and one back to Nazareth, (Luke 2:39) after Simeon and Anna's prophetic confirmation, utterances and Mary's purification (Luke 2:22-24).

Three Wise Men

Here's what I thought I knew: There were three wise men visiting baby Yeshua in Bethlehem while He lay in the manger; each bearing a gift of gold, frankincense or myrrh. Even our nativity scenes depict three kings or wise men bringing gifts.

Here's more to consider: The Bible does not say the wise men visited baby Yeshua in Bethlehem, or that there were three of them, or that they were wise.

The term "wise men" is translated from the word "magi," which means "astronomer or observer of the clouds." These Eastern astronomers didn't even know that Yeshua was being born in Bethlehem until the night they observed His star in the west (Matt. 2:2). So, it stands to reason that they did not begin to travel west to search for the King of the Jews until some point after Yeshua was born and the star had been seen. It may have taken from six months to over a year and hundreds of miles for the magi to actually locate the young child in Nazareth.

Scripture tells us the magi came to Joseph and Mary's house in Nazareth and saw the young "child" (Matt. 2:11). Joseph and Mary were back in Nazareth, and Yeshua was not an infant anymore. Joseph and Mary had only traveled to Bethlehem from Nazareth, which is approximately 70 miles, because of Caesar Augustus' decree (Luke 2:1).

History tells us that these magi used to travel in groups of up to three hundred people. The number of wise men has become three simply because of the number of gifts they brought. Daniel had spent time in Babylon centuries earlier, could these magi have been the Chaldeans or astrologers (Dan. 4:7) who had kept record of Daniel's predictions for centuries?

There is a reason we commonly have three wise men shown in our nativity scenes today. When St. Francis of Assisi arranged the first nativity scene, he used townspeople like actors to stand shifts and pose as the characters. It looked rather empty to St. Francis with just Joseph, Mary, baby Yeshua, a couple shepherds and a few farm animals posing for onlookers. (Francis knew the wise men did not belong there) Then St. Francis decided to add the three wise men to help fill out the stage. The big church in Rome has even gone so far as to make up names for the "supposed" three wise men; Gaspar, Melchior and Balthasar.

Shortly after the magi departed, Joseph had the dream telling him to take Mary and Yeshua and flee to Egypt (Matt. 2:13). In that day, Egypt was a rather expensive place to live. So the gifts of gold, frankincense and myrrh may very well have financed their stay.

Hem of His Garment

Here's what I thought I knew: The woman had to reach to the ground or by the Lord's ankles in order to touch the hem of His robe (garment) for healing of her 12 year ailment (Mark 5:27).

Here's more to consider: What we are talking about here is the garment from which we now see as the Jewish prayer shawl. The shawl is called a Tallit (pronounced tal-eet) and means "little tent." It has fringes on each end and tassels with a blue thread interwoven in the knots on each corner (Num. 15:37-40). This is symbolic of the tent Tabernacle that Israel had in the wilderness. Anytime someone wanted to pray, they could pull the tallit up over their head and have a symbolic tent Tabernacle to commune with the Lord in privacy. Though slightly different in design, being a garment open on the sides back then, this would be the prayer closet Yeshua spoke of in (Matt. 6:6) and (Luke 12:3). When the head was covered, this would symbolically keep the "spirit of the world" outside and one could pray undistracted, without being double-minded (James 1:7, 8).

The tassel is called a Tzitzit. The Tzitzit strings are usually tied in knots totaling 613, symbolic of the Torah (Law of Moses). There is a techelet (blue) thread woven in the Tzitzit knots.

The origin of the tallit might be a symbolic reminder about keeping the purity of the camp (Num. 15:32-36). A guy had just been caught gathering firewood on the Sabbath. They did not know what to do with him. God said to stone him to death outside the camp. While possibly unassociated events, it seems the next thing God instructed them to do was make the tallit; to remember the commandments of the Lord and to do them (Num. 15:39, 40).

The tallit is what the Lord was poking fun at the Pharisees about, when he spoke of them making extra-long fringes (Matt. 23:5). The fringe or tassel on His tallit is what the woman touched for healing (Matt. 9:20) (Luke 8:43, 44). Why did she (Mark 5:33) come trembling? She would have been ritually unclean according to the Torah/Law of Moses. To touch anyone, especially a rabbi, would have brought severe reprimand.

When the Lord was in villages, cities or the country, the sick besought him that they might touch the fringe, tassels or hem of his garment and were healed (Matt. 14:36) (Mark 6:56).

Different translations of the Bible use the terms "hem or border of His garment, edge of His cloak, fringes and some even use tassels" for the above verses. This would be the mantle (ornamental covering) that Elijah passed on to Elisha. This is the same mantle both Elijah and Elisha used to part the Jordan River (2 Kings 2:8, 14). The four corners of the Tallit can also be called "wings." This symbolizes us being under the protective wings of the Lord. (Psalms 91) Scripture also tells us Messiah comes with healing in His wings (Mal. 4:2). The same Hebrew word translated "corners" in (Num. 15:38) is interchangeably translated "wings" in (Mal. 4:2).

Was Jesus a Pacifist?

Here's what I thought I knew: Jesus Christ was a quiet, gentle, meek and mild, easy going, soft spoken pacifist.

Here's more to consider: Just because of the love of God, we have a tendency to view Him as a comfortable family member. We must remember He is still the God who judges.

A mellow easy going guy does not braid up some rope, knock over many people's tables of money and whip the group out of the Temple all by Himself (John 2:15).

A soft spoken kind of a guy does not avoid arrest because of the authoritative manner in which He speaks (John 7:44-46). A pacifist kind of a guy does not instruct His followers to take money and go buy swords (Luke 22:36-38).

A quiet reserved kind of a guy does not go in front of the biggest religious leaders of the day and claim to be the Lord God of Israel, knowing beforehand they will eventually kill Him for it (John 8:56-58). A timid kind of a guy is not the Holy Judge of all mankind (2 Tim. 4:1).

A meek guy does not take control of demons so powerful they can make 2,000 swine drown themselves (Mark 5:13). A gentle soft spoken kind of a guy does not astonish people with the power of His Word (Luke 4:32, 36).

A mild sort of guy does not come to divide (Luke 12:51-53). A mellow friendly kind of a guy does not call the biggest religious leaders of the day, to their face in front of a crowd, "offspring of the serpent" (Matt. 12:34). A soft spoken kind of a guy does not keep crowds of 4,000 to 10,000 people riveted so intently all day long that nobody wants to leave and He has to feed them dinner (Mark 6:34-44) (Mark 8:1-9).

A quiet sensitive kind of a guy does not tell the biggest religious leaders (Matt 21:16) to their face, in front of a crowd, "have ye not read (the Scripture)?" Some Pharisees had the whole Torah memorized. An easy going kind of a guy does not scold the biggest preachers of the day, in front of a crowd, "ye do err, not knowing the Scriptures" (Matt. 22:29).

The Lord coming as a Peacemaker who loves and forgives us might make Him a pacifist in your mind. But, Yeshua the Messiah is still the Lord, the God and the Judge of all mankind and a very predominant Presence.

The Elijah that is to Come

Here's what I thought I knew: "Behold, I will send you Elijah the prophet before the great and dreadful day of the Lord" (Malachi 4:5). This verse implies Elijah is one of the Two Witnesses in (Rev. 11:3).

Here's more to consider: This misapplication is usually part of the Pre-Tribulation Rapture theory. Yeshua made a specific point to say that John the Baptist "was" the Elijah that was to come (Matt. 11:14) (Matt. 17:11-13). John was not Elijah reincarnated. He preached with the same steadfast and no compromise spirit that Elijah had done previously.

Mary Magdalene a Prostitute?

Here's what I thought I knew: Mary Magdalene was a former prostitute who traveled with and served the Lord. Some even imply she was the well-known madam of Magdala.

Here's more to consider: The Bible does not contain one verse that says Mary Magdalene was a prostitute. It says she had seven demons cast out of her (Luke 8:2).

Did Yeshua Carry the Cross?

Here's what I thought I knew: After a beating and scourging, it is traditionally taught and Hollywood movies also portray that Yeshua carried the cross. They show that He fell beneath it three times before Simon the Cyrenian offered to help.

Here's more to consider: The Bible does not say Yeshua carried the cross at all. He bore our transgressions "on" the cross. This is a case where tradition has taken over the facts. Scripture says the cross (or cross-bar) was placed or forced on Simon the Cyrenian (Matt. 27:32) (Mark 15:21) (Luke 23:26). John only uses pronouns to describe this event (John 19:17). The "he" (Simon) bearing His (Yeshua's) own cross, went forth to a place called Golgotha. It is obvious in John's account, the "he" bearing the cross; bore it all the way to the place of the skull. If Yeshua were the "he" bearing it all the way to Golgotha, this would make us wonder when Simon had been enlisted to help. This would also contradict the other three accounts. If Yeshua were to have carried the cross; it would have been for the first part of the trek and not the final distance to Golgotha. After a scourging, Yeshua was likely physically incapable of carrying anything; which is why the cross was put on Simon from the start. So, when you see people carry crosses around, they are imitating Simon the Cyrenian and not Messiah!

Good Friday?

Here's what I thought I knew: Messiah was crucified on Friday.

Here's more to consider: Even with counting a portion of a day as a day, which is a legitimate Hebrew manner of count; there is no way to get three days and three nights in the grave with a Friday crucifixion (Matt. 12:39, 40).

The Lord and the disciples were eating the Passover meal after Wednesday sundown. Later, they went to the garden, Yeshua was arrested, tried, convicted, sentenced and scourged in the early hours. He was on the cross from 9 am to 3 pm and in a nearby tomb before sundown Thursday, and still Passover.

What day (Lev. 23:4-8) always follows Passover? Sundown Thursday ended Passover and began the first day of the week long Feast of Unleavened Bread. This would involve two full days and two full nights, plus a portion of a day and a portion of a night, to be three days and three nights in the grave.

When sundown Thursday occurred and Passover was complete, the first day of Unleavened Bread began, which no work could be done. Sundown Friday would have begun the normal weekly Sabbath, which no work could be done, and the reason nobody returned to the tomb before sundown on Saturday. This time frame would negate the likelihood of a Friday crucifixion.

Side Note: You will find in history, that after the Babylonian captivity, there was a widespread and accepted combining of Passover and the first day of Unleavened Bread as the same day, but it was not like that previous to the captivity.

Shroud of Turin

Here's what I thought I knew: Since the 1300's, the big church in Rome claims to have the burial cloth Yeshua was wrapped in after the crucifixion.

Here's more to consider: The carbon dating tests report it was from the middle ages. The forensic expert who examined the shroud on TV concluded the image on the cloth was a 5'11" Caucasian male. Shouldn't it be a Jewish male image? If it was the sheet He was transported in, wouldn't the image have been smeared in travel from the cross to the tomb?

Does the Lord want His people to line up for miles, waiting to worship His burial cloth? Isn't that idolatry? Why would the Vatican embrace this shroud for centuries, allow people to idolize the shroud, be hesitant to allow any experts to examine it and then decline to comment on the authenticity of the shroud?

Joseph and Nicodemus took about 100 lbs. of myrrh, spices and linen strips to wrap Yeshua's body (John 19:39, 40), like the Egyptians used to do with mummies. The Jews would not wrap the head as such, but used a different method with a napkin. Myrrh, a sap that begins to harden when it meets the air, was applied to the linen strips and would have become like a hardened 100 lb. cocoon in the shape of the body. Remember, the Lord told them to remove these same wrappings (grave clothes or linen strips) when Lazarus had been raised from the dead (John 11:44).

When the disciples entered the tomb, they probably saw the grave clothes hardened in the shape of the Lord's body, without the body in it; while the head wrap was rolled or folded and separately placed. They knew it was impossible to remove the body without destroying the stiff shell (wrappings), yet it was intact and undisturbed. They saw, understood and believed the Lord had risen (John 20:8). That would convince me too!

Jewish eating customs would indicate the napkin being neatly folded meant the Master was to "return" to the table to finish His meal. If the napkin were crumpled up in a pile, that would mean He was finished and would not be returning.

God Heareth not Sinners?

Here's what I thought I knew: "Now we know that God heareth not sinners" (John 9:31). Of course this means the Lord does not hear the prayers of a sinner.

Here's more to consider: At first glance, this statement "seems" to make sense and appears to be true. But, who is actually speaking? These were the words of the blind man (to whom Jesus had restored sight) when he was defending his miraculous healing to the Pharisees (John 9:30). This statement was not written by a Spirit filled disciple, nor was it intended to be turned into doctrine. Secondly, if God never heard sinners, where would that leave us? How would anybody be able to come to a conversion experience if the Lord did not hear a sinner cry out to Him (Job 35:12) with a repentant heart?

By His Stripes

Here's what I thought I knew: (Isa. 53:5) and (1 Peter 2:24) have some great biblical significance connected with miraculous physical healing. All you need is enough faith, claim that the stripes Yeshua took were for your bodily restoration, and you'll be healed. There are even some who would go so far as to imply that Yeshua took 39 stripes and there are 39 main human physical diseases. So, He took a stripe for each and every disease, thus defeating all sickness of mankind.

Here's more to consider: First of all, there is no verse that states how many times Yeshua was scourged. It was Paul who took the 39 lashes or "forty save one," 5 different times (2 Cor. 11:24). This number was a Roman punishment upon a Roman citizen, and there may have been no rules about how many lashes could be given to a non-Roman citizen. There are nine times in the whole book of Isaiah that some form or tense of the word "heal" is used. When you read these verses, (and the verses surrounding them) it becomes apparent that Isaiah is only speaking about spiritual healing or "the atonement for sin." Though the Lord can and does heal our bodies; not one of these verses pertains to healing of the physical body whatsoever.

(Isaiah 3:7) (Isaiah 6:10) (Isaiah 19:22) (Isaiah 30:26) (Isaiah 53:5) (Isaiah 57:18, 19) (Isaiah 58:8)

When you read the rest of the verse, Peter is obviously speaking of the salvation of our souls and the atonement for sin (1 Peter 2:24). Peter had spent years with the Lord as an eye witness to many peoples' bodily healing. He was not referring to the physical in this case, but to the spiritual atonement. This was a letter of instruction, encouragement and admonition from Peter to fellow believers in Asia Minor. There is no doubt the Lord can heal us at any time; but do you really think Peter intended to have a portion of one sentence from a letter (taken out of its original context) to be turned into a magic incantation supposedly motivating God to heal our physical body?

Were 120 People in an Upper Room?

Here's what I thought I knew: There were 120 people in an upper room on the day of Pentecost when they were filled with the Ruach Hakodesh (Holy Spirit) (Acts 2:1-4).

Here's more to consider: It does not say there were 120 people in an upper room anywhere in Acts Chapter 2. This thought is taken from the previous chapter where the people numbered were "about 120," to elect Matthias as the replacement disciple for Judas (Acts 1:15-26). The number required to assemble a Jewish council is usually about 120. This may explain the count of men. After the Lord ascended, the disciples continued to meet in the Temple (Luke 24:53). Where were they on the day

71

of Shavuot (Pentecost)? Why would thousands of Jews (some with different languages) travel to Jerusalem from great distances to be gathered in an "upper room"? If there were still about 120 believers in a group, wouldn't they be worshiping in the Jewish Temple to commemorate the giving of the Torah to Moses on Mt. Sinai? They had been instructed to linger in Jerusalem, not necessarily to stay cooped up in an upper room. This celebration of Shavuot (now called Pentecost) was 50 days after Passover.

Side Note: The Israelites ate the Passover meal 50 days before God gave Moses the Torah (Law) on Mt. Sinai. Yeshua was the Passover Lamb 50 days before the day of Shavuot (Pentecost). And if you notice, 3,000 people were slain in (Exod. 32:28); and 3,000 people were saved in (Acts 2:41).

Acts Chapter 2 starts a completely new thought and a completely different day from chapter one. It says, "When the day of Shavuot was fully come, they were all in one accord in one place." Then a rushing mighty wind filled the whole house. The same Greek word "oikos" that is translated "house" in (Acts 2:2) was translated "Temple" in (Luke 11:51). The Temple is called the "house" (oikos) of God in numerous passages (Matt. 21:13) (Mark 2:26, 11:17) (Luke 6:4, 19:46).

Did the 3,000 people baptized that day also fit into an upper room? But wait, there were more than 3,000 people, because some did not receive the Word that day (Acts 2:41). A place large enough to hold the 3,000 or more people present that day was the Jewish Temple. Beside the huge hall, there were side rooms that could hold thousands of people. The Temple ceremonial washing pools were useable for all the baptisms.

This day of Shavuot (Pentecost) story in Acts Chapter Two ends by talking about how this group continued to meet "at the Temple" day by day (Acts 2:46). Then Acts Chapter Three begins with them in the Temple again. Being in the Jewish Temple for the special Jewish day of Shavuot would not be unusual for Jewish disciples.

CHAPTER FOUR

Was Lucifer ever the Name of the Devil?

Here's what I thought I knew: The devil was once the chief angel named Lucifer; who was in charge of the heavenly choir or band. Lucifer was kicked out of heaven for wanting to be equal to or above God.

Here's more to consider: There is nothing in the Bible that says the devil was ever an angel, or that his name was ever Lucifer. The word "lucifer" wasn't even in the Bible until after 400 AD! In Hebrew "Ha Satan" is not even a proper name, but a term that has become a name. It means adversary and accuser, describing one who opposes.

Isaiah Chapter 14

We must begin by noticing all of Isaiah chapter 14 is a taunting speech or poetic prophecy about the downfall of the king of Babylon, and not the devil (Isa. 14:4). The one to whom this is written is a man (the king of Babylon) and not a fallen angel named Lucifer (Isa. 14:16).

The location of this prophecy is the city is Babylon, not heaven. The time of this prophecy is hundreds of years before Messiah, not a time frame before Adam.

The word "lucifer" was never originally in the Bible (Isa. 14:12). In 405 AD, Jerome translated the Hebrew and Greek into Latin (the Vulgate). The Hebrew word "heylel" carries a meaning of "brightness" (symbolic of the morning star). Jerome translated this word "heylel" into lucifer.

The King James translators did not translate "heylel." They just reused the word "lucifer" from Jerome's Latin, because it still meant the same thing at that time. Then in 1667, John Milton wrote a fictional (that means made up) book "Paradise Lost." This book depicts "Lucifer" as an angel that sinned and was

73

thrown out of heaven. The two ideas have grown together over time to the point where the misunderstanding is more widespread than the truth. Webster's Dictionary defines "lucifer" as a match ignited by means of friction (as in a dark room), but not as the devil's name. None of the Old Testament prophets, the disciples, Paul or Yeshua Himself believed that a being by the name of "Lucifer" was cast out of heaven and became the devil we read about in Scripture.

You will find that many Bible translations have discovered this error about (Isa. 14:12) and removed the word "lucifer." One Bible translates "O morning star, son of the dawn." Another Bible says "O Day Star, son of Dawn." Young's Concordance uses "shining one." The Bible never states anywhere that Lucifer was the name of the devil, or that he was ever an angel.

Most of Isaiah Chapter 14 is full of figures of speech used to tease the king of Babylon (verse 4). His ego is taunted, his pride was crumbling and his kingdom destroyed. Is this the "man" who caused fear, (Isa. 14:16) or turned the land into a desert? There is nothing about the accuser (Ha Satan) here.

Ezekiel Chapter 28
Another place that has been taken out of context and incorrectly attributed to the devil is Ezekiel Chapter 28. The subject is the King of Tyre, not Satan (Ezek. 28:2, 12). Notice the previous Chapter 27 has been about Tyre also. There is no mention of a fallen angel there either.

The location of this prophecy is the wealthy city of Tyre, and not heaven. The time frame of this prophecy is the 6th century BC, and not a time before human history began. The ruler of Tyre (Tyrus) had become proud and though a mere man, thought of himself as a god (Ezek. 28:2). Even his wealth (Ezek. 28:3-5) and wisdom wouldn't save him from his ultimate demise and destruction (Ezek. 28:18, 19).

The "wisdom" spoken of, was the understanding to know how to make money, riches and treasures (Ezek. 28:4, 5). It was by his "traffic" or commercial trading that his riches were increased. The "terrible of the nations" (Ezek. 28:7) were the armies of Nebuchadnezzar, King of Babylon (Ezek. 30:10, 11). Nothing about the devil here either.

The precious stones adorning the king of Tyre (Ezek. 28:13) were available from trading with countries that offered "all kinds of spices, precious stones and gold" (Ezek. 27:22). Did the devil trade with other countries for stones he could be adorned with? Why would Satan need gold in his pocket? Doesn't the devil use the temptation of riches to distract souls?

The king of Tyre was called "perfect in beauty" (Ezek. 28:12). There is no reason to think this is about Satan before a supposed fall from heaven. The city of Jerusalem is said to be "perfect in beauty" (Ezek. 16:14). Tyre is said to be perfect in beauty (Ezek. 27:3). The hanging shields on the walls made "thy beauty perfect" (Ezek. 27:11). The word "perfect" doesn't mean sinless, it describes a wholeness or completeness. When was Ha-Satan ever called "perfect or beautiful"?

Keep in mind the king of Tyre wasn't a "perfect being." It says he was "perfect in his ways" (Ezek. 28:15). He was perfect in his ways as a leader and king, until iniquity was found in him. The "iniquity" is in merchandising (traffic) or dishonest trading and selling practices (Ezek. 28:18). This is not about the devil's iniquity for deceiving Eve.

Thou art the anointed cherub that covereth (Ezek. 28:14). Ezekiel described cherubim in (Ezek. 10) as having four wings and four faces, and is not talking about a "fallen angel" in this passage. The king (one who covers or leads) was the protector of the people of Tyre. This writing is "sarcastic" poetic license, and not a statement referring to Ha-Satan. Ridicule or sarcasm means the opposite of the words used. Michal said to David, "How glorious was the king today?" (2 Sam. 6:20) She clearly did not think he was glorious, (2 Sam. 6:16) she despised him.

Back when Elijah mocked the Baal prophets, he said, "Cry aloud, for he is a god" (1 Kings 18:27). He did not mean Baal was a god. Nor did he think calling louder would do them any good. It was sarcasm! Ezekiel 28 has many uses of sarcasm. Thou hast said "I am a god, I sit in the seat of the gods (Verse 2), thou art wiser than Daniel (Verse 3), there is no secret they can hide from thee (Verse 3), thou hast been in Eden (Verse 13), thou art the anointed cherub that covers (Verse 14) and you were upon the holy mountain of God (Verse 14).

Of course, the true meaning would be the opposite. He is not a god. He is not wiser than Daniel. Secrets can be hidden from him. He was not in the garden with Adam. He was not a cherub or upon the holy mountain of God. This grand speech is still talking exclusively about the king of Tyre. He was a man who set his heart as the heart of God (Ezek.28:2). When is the devil ever referred to as a "man" in the Bible?

What about the King of Tyre (Ezek. 28:13), actually visiting the land of Eden? It is one of the countries the king of Tyre had been doing trade with (Ezek. 27:23). Since trade had been carried on with the land of Eden, it is not improbable the king of Tyre could have actually visited Eden himself, back in 600 BC. This has nothing to do with Ha-Satan and a garden "in" the land of Eden, way back in Adam and Eve's time.

Satan's fall in the book of Luke?
There is another passage sometimes linked with the "devil's fall" (Luke 10:18). Yeshua says, "I beheld Satan as lightening fall from heaven."

The seventy disciples had just returned from a successful preaching mission. With joy they reported that even the devils are subject to them through the Lord's name (Luke 10:17). The sick were being healed, the blind gained sight, the lame walked, and the devils were being cast out. The disciples were surprised about what just took place. The context says nothing about Satan's fall before Adam and Eve. This was happening at that moment.

For example, Capernaum was exalted to heaven and would be thrust down to hell, signifying a fall from its exalted position (Luke 10:15). Yeshua saw that Ha-Satan's power was quickly and presently being crushed, as lightening from heaven. The Lord was stating that Satan was being brought down low from a place of arrogance and control. The aorist tense of the word "fall" brings a meaning of present and continual fall, and not pertaining to an incident that happened before Adam.

In conclusion, we find:
(Isaiah 14) is exclusively about the pride, arrogance, and fall of the king of Babylon in his time; and says nothing about a fallen angel before the Garden in Eden. The Bible does not say that Lucifer was Ha-Satan's name; nor is Ha-Satan an official name, but a term that became a name. The Bible never says Ha-Satan was the number one archangel or cherubim. Translation and man's tradition have brought this concept about.

(Ezekiel 28) is exclusively about the king of Tyre in his day and not about an angel or cherubim falling before creation.
(Luke 10:18) is an observation about the fall of Ha-Satan's dominion in Yeshua's day, and not about a time frame before Adam. If John Milton had not written "Paradise Lost," we would not even be having this conversation.
(John 9:5) We all know Messiah is the Light of the world, so isn't it a conflict of interest to call Satan, the "light-bearer"?
(John 8:44) Yeshua said the devil was a murderer from the beginning. Would that mean Lucifer was a murdering angel?
(1 John 3:8) The disciple John said the devil has sinned from the beginning. This is hardly angelic behavior.

Do you see how man's tradition has taken precedence over the actual Scripture? The Russian leader Lenin once said that a lie told often enough becomes the truth. Scripture never says Ha-Satan ever led worship, the heavenly band or choir either. This imaginary description stems from John Milton's made up story.

It is amusing to ponder that anyone who thinks they worship the devil by calling him "Lucifer," is using a Latin word that was not translated into English; and it is biblically and historically inaccurate for the devil. And by calling him Satan, they're using a word from the Bible, and the very God they try to deny exists!

Christmas and Easter

Here's what I thought I knew: Even though the origins of the winter (Christmas) and spring (Easter) solstice festivals are pagan, that isn't what it means to us today. We do it now for Jesus! Just because there are suspicious origins associated with these traditions, we don't want to disappoint the children by telling them not to incorporate former pagan activities and observances into their worship. And we celebrate the death, burial and resurrection of the Lord like everybody else; by telling our kids a giant bunny hid some chocolate eggs for them to find.

Here's more to consider: Think about that statement, "We do it now for Jesus." As we continue to "do it" now for Jesus, are we actually repeating a Babylonian pagan sun god ritual for Jesus?

Do you really think taking pagan things and attaching Bible significance to them, is proper in the Lord's eyes? If the pagans had not used trees, you never would have thought to chop down a tree on Dec. 25th.

Why would the traditional meal of a Jewish Messiah's birthday be "ham"? Pork was on the unclean list of banned foods. Does traditional boar's head soup have anything to do with the old Nimrod mythology as well? Look it up for yourself.

When I was a kid, the understood "bad side" of Christmas was the materialism. As long as we kept our focus off the money and the stuff, then we could enjoy all the money and the stuff.

Then I began to wonder; if this is Messiah's birthday, why do we give presents to each other? What does the Lord get out of that? And to "whom" are we thankful?

Then I wondered if Santa Claus is just the fat clown at the wrong birthday party; and why does Santa get more presentation, adoration and focus than the Lord?

Then I wondered; if Christmas and Easter are Christian holidays, why do so many non-believers celebrate Christmas and Easter?

Then I wondered; if this is a special occasion for the Lord, why do we chop down a couple billion of His beautiful trees, just to throw them in the trash weeks later? What does the Lord get out of that?

Then I wondered; how does it benefit the Lord when a family overspends for Christmas, putting themselves in debt and hardship for months to come? Is this good stewardship?

Then I wondered why people would put crosses on Christmas trees. Isn't it poor taste to remind baby Messiah of His coming sacrificial destiny, on His very birthday?

Then I wondered if they only made fruit bread that one year. Because nobody ever eats it, they just re-wrap it and send it to someone else next year!

Volumes are already filled with the pagan origins of these supposed Christian holidays and all the other aspects that go along with them; which the big church in Rome chose to absorb, rather than outlaw. We encourage you to do at least a little investigation, and get your kids involved too. See how the Lord convicts your heart as you learn about these observances.

For starters, research biblical names such as: Ashtaroth or Ashtoreth, Asherah poles, prophets of the groves, the triad deity Baal, Mithraism and Saturnalia worship, Nimrod and his boar hunting accident, and Santa Claus or St. Nicholas too. When you see the name "Semiramus" appear; remember she really lived around 800 BC. Over the years she and Nimrod (2000 BC?) have been combined and associated together. Gee, just like evergreen trees and eggs and bunnies and Jesus!

Your research should include the baking of round cakes to the Queen of Heaven (Jer. 44:16-19, 25), weeping 40 days for Tammuz (Ezek. 8:14), the mother and child cult of Babylon and the origins of Easter eggs and Christmas trees. Back in Babylon, they had Baal temple prostitutes but, the priests had to remain celibate. Where do we see priestly celibacy today? You'll be surprised, if not shocked.

Almost 100 years ago, the preacher H.A. Ironside wrote, "But when (Lent, Good Friday, Easter, Christ's Mass) are turned into church festivals, they certainly come under the condemnation of (Gal. 4:9-11)... All of them and many more are Babylonish in their origin and were at one time linked with the Ashtoreth and Tammuz mystery worship. It is through Rome that they come down to us." ("Revelation" 1920, H.A. Ironside, page 301)

It is worth noting that the Mid-East culture does not honor a great person on their birthday, but on their death day. Why don't we put up a tree in April, May or on the 4th of July? Why doesn't anybody put up a tree a little closer to when He really would have been born, maybe in September?

Even the name "Christ's Mass" lets you know the big church in Rome blesses and promotes it. Are we daughters of Mother Rome (Rev. 17)? Do we carry her theology, traditions and doctrines? Do we revere her idols, relics and observe her blasphemous practices? The early church never entertained such nonsense as trees and eggs and bunnies.

In "The Popes against the Jews" (by David Kertzer, page 74), Rabbis in the ghettos of Rome were forced to wear clownish outfits and march through the streets to jeers and pelting of whatever was thrown. As late as 1836, Pope Gregory XVI was petitioned by the Jews, to stop the Saturnalia abuse of the Jewish community. He saw no reason for any innovation or change.

Did you know the Pilgrims had a law around the year 1620, lasting for decades; forbidding Christmas trees? They had just vacated Europe to get away from the papacy and to find religious freedom in America. They wanted to keep papal idols and observances out of their Christian worship here in America.

Yes, the word "Easter" is in the King James Bible (Acts 12:4).

The terms spring, Easter and Passover had become interchangeable 400 years ago. They used the word "Easter" to convey that it was spring time, the Passover season. Most other translations use the word Passover (from the Greek: pascha). If the pagans had never used sunrise services, eaten fish on Friday, honored eggs and bunnies (fertility symbols) at the spring solstice; you would never have associated eggs and bunnies with the resurrection of the Lord. If the pagans had never baked round cakes to the Queen of heaven, you would not see hot cross buns only around Easter (Jer. 7:18, 28, 30). Early Catholic missionaries were unable to stop the people from baking the round cakes in the spring. They compromised and blessed the round cakes by putting a cross on them, "now" making them holy and acceptable. Even the maypole stems from ancient fertility rites, now also enacted as pole dancing.

If pagans had not burned yuletide logs with astrological signs on them, you would never have thought to do so on the Lord's birthday. If the pagans had never hung round things on a tree to pay homage to their sun god, you would not have thought of hanging ornaments on a tree for Jesus. The nativity of the sun festival stems from long before Messiah was born.

Although the weeping 40 days for Tammuz was formerly a summer observance, it seems to have evolved into what is called "Lent" today (Ezek. 8:14). Does mourning for 40 days help make the Easter observance happen each year? Sunrise services have their beginnings from Babylon and sun god worship, which was long before Messiah. We see past artists using a halo (nimbus) in religious artwork, and even the eating of fish on Friday stems from pagan worship.

If pagans had never revered some goddess's tears, you never would have thought to hang mistletoe at Christmas time. If the pagans never had snake cults, you would not have thought to use garland on your tree or thresholds. If the pagans never had wreaths, you would not have thought to hang one on your door. Garland (meaning wreath) is mentioned as an adornment on oxen for sacrifice by the priest of Jupiter (Zeus) (Acts 14:13). Compromise usually begins this way: Oh, but that isn't what it means to us today. Do you think it really matters to God what you think this pagan observance has evolved into, or what you "think" it means to you today? That would be like YHVH rubbing His hands with worry because some dyslexic atheist doesn't believe there is a dog! God's feelings on the subject of absorbing other religious activities seem to be the same throughout the Bible and here are a few examples:

You are to burn them with fire (Deut. 7:5).
Do not even bring it into your house (Deut. 7:25, 26).
You shall not do so unto the Lord your God (Deut. 12:2-4).
Do not inquire how others serve their gods (Deut. 12:30-32).
This is the punishment for such observances (Deut. 17:2-5).
John said to "keep yourselves from idols" (1 John 5:21).

If private school boys hadn't discovered they could get larger gifts by writing flowery letters home just before Christmas, you would not have thought to send Christmas cards.

Had St. Francis of Assisi never added three wise men to the first nativity scene, you would not have the wise men in yours. The wise men were not there when Yeshua was born. The elusive "good will among men" feeling that accompanies the giving at Christmas time, is what we as believers should be exhibiting all year round. Why should this "caring" only be evident at Christmas time? Why can't you care for your fellow man for the rest of the year without a tree in your living room?

What do you think you are missing if you don't have a tree or eggs? Are you teaching your children to mindlessly follow erroneous doctrines and pagan traditions without question? Do you think the Lord is impressed with how pretty your tree is, or how well you color eggs?

For an experiment one year, try releasing yourself from the bondage of wasting money on trees, special wrapping paper, lights, decor and ornaments. Avoid the egg coloring kits, the mess and fuss, the disappointment of the wrong gift, late gifts or not getting a gift at all. Avoid spending too much out of obligation. Do you remember the relief you feel when it's all over? And the work of putting it all away, so you can do it all over again next year?

Try to open your conscience and your heart to the insight and understanding the Lord reveals to you. But beware; you will be surprised at the reactions you will observe from those around you. More than once I have heard the words, "You believe in God and you don't do Christmas? What's wrong with you?"

If you were living 2,000 years ago, would you have done this garbage in front of the Lord? Would you have a tree if you were face to face with Yeshua? Do you expect your judgment to be less severe for having trees and eggs, and teaching your children to compromise also? These pagan traditions had been in place long before Messiah came. It makes you wonder who the reason for the season was before Yeshua was born.

As in Moses and Jeremiah's day, there was trouble with the people incorporating pagan worship into the Jewish worship (Psalms 106:32-36). They did not abandon their own religion; they were polluting it with outside ungodly doctrines, observances and activity. There isn't much new under the sun, is there?

Huge amounts of information in history books, encyclopedias and other church sources are available on the Mithraism and Saturnalia observances. These things are no secret and we encourage you to research and verify it for yourself. Should we Christians continue to perpetuate ancient Babylonian and pagan Roman Catholic traditions "in the name of Jesus"?

Halloween

I'm not even going to use my usual format for this one. It's wrong; you have the choice...so don't do it. Go ahead and research the origins of Trick or Treat, Samhain, Halloween, and All Hallows Eve to learn the trashy beginnings. It does not matter to God if you think it means something else today.

Side Note: Did you know Martin Luther nailed his 95 Thesis to the door of All Saint's Church on Oct. 31, 1517? Now the day after Halloween is called "All Saint's Day."

We have our spineless fellow believers who "won't" take part in Halloween anymore. It's because they found out it is wrong. Now they have a "Harvest Day Festival" on Oct. 31, for an alternative to Halloween. Instead of evil costumes, they encourage their children to dress up like Bible characters. Then they use the church to bob for Christian apples and trick or treat for Christian candy. Pathetic! Am I the only one to see the compromise here? I would think the Lord would hate the compromise more than the stupid holiday.

What do you think you are missing if you don't do Halloween? Will you "proudly" stand before the Lord on Judgment day to say as an adult, you mindlessly continued to dress up for Halloween and taught your children to do likewise? Even just sitting at home and giving out candy is still taking part in it.

The Virgin Mary and Catholicism

Here's what I thought I knew: Not only does Rome demand you believe that Mary is an eternal virgin, but they want you to believe she is co-redeemer with Jesus. They also believe that Joseph and Mary's mother are eternal virgins. If you do not believe this, you are accursed. (Vatican 2 Council Decisions)

Here's more to consider: Oh yes, Mary was a virgin until she had given birth. It says that Joseph took Mary as wife and knew her not until Yeshua was born (Matt. 1:25). Then surely he knew her and she was a virgin no longer. If you recall, Mary was betrothed to Joseph for a while. Even though no marital relations took place, Mary had every intention to not be a virgin for very much longer. Do you think Joseph expected Mary to be an eternal virgin after the marriage took place?

I just don't know what to say about Joseph and Mary's mother being eternal virgins. Maybe I do. They must have taken that right out of the Bible, because it is not in there now! Why would I be accursed if I don't believe Joseph and Mary's mother are eternal virgins? Do you think Joseph or Mary's mother expected to be called an eternal virgin?

Do you realize that the term "you are accursed" gave the papacy the right to kill all the "heretics" in the past? It is still in print today and they have not changed a word of it. They have chosen not to use that option of late, but it is still as valid and current today as it was in the past. Lately, they use honey instead of vinegar to bring who they formerly called heretics, now softly coined "separated brethren," back into their fold. Now, they even have a TV commercial hailing all Catholics to come home. And why are Catholics now called Christians, which originally was Rome's "derogatory label" for followers of Messiah? Rome persecuted and killed Jews and Christians for centuries, including Protestants.

There are a number of unusual things required to be believed in the Vatican 2 Council Decisions, and many end with the conclusion; if you do not believe what we say, you are accursed. There are many good people (wanting to serve God) being deceived by the teachings of Catholicism. After all the generations that have known this and voiced it (to their peril), you would think Rome might try to change and be more in line with what the Bible says, huh?

Rome teaches, once the priest blesses the bread for communion, it becomes the "Eucharist." This means the actual true body of the Lord to them. Wouldn't that be considered cannibalism? (The Lord said to do this in remembrance of Him, it is symbolic!) But, if you don't believe the bread and wine are His actual body and blood, according to them, you are accursed. This gives them the duty to put you to death for heresy (Vatican 2 Council Decisions). The thin round wafers (round cakes) you've seen served for communion with "IHS" stamped on it, are man perpetuated continuations which have symbolic ties to the old Babylon sun worship.

85

Unfortunately, you cannot study the Bible without learning a little something about Rome. It was in power back then and still is today, under a different guise. Did the early church understand from Daniel's prophecy that the little horn would be more terrible and ferocious (in a different capacity) than its predecessor? This little horn, still ruling and reigning from Rome, would take Rome's place and be the seat of Spiritual impurity that would devour (spread throughout) the earth.

The big church in Rome has had 1,500 years to spread her heresies, false doctrines, idolatry, traditions and observances around the world. The "Immaculate Conception" teaches that Mary (not Yeshua) was born sinless and is the mother of God. They say she is co-redeemer, she was taken to heaven without dying a human death, and was crowned the Queen of heaven. And technically, her name was Miriam, and not Mary! They have invented purgatory, sold indulgences, taught the soul exists apart from the body after death, and re-written the Ten Commandments to exclude the one forbidding idolatry; now they have two about coveting. They have changed the Sabbath from Saturday to Sunday, changed the crucifixion from Wednesday or Thursday to Friday; and even re-written the identity of the Jewish God, saying "YHVH" is three separate individual persons and Jesus Christ is one of them! And if they believe Mary is the mother of God, and their Catholic god is a trinity; that means Mary is the mother of the Father, and of the Son, and of the Holy Spirit. Do you see the confusion here?

Many Protestant denominations carry enough teachings from Babylon and Rome that they are basically "Catholic light"! We should be educated, discerning and able to refute contradictions and unsound doctrine (Titus 1:9). And why do we think Constantine knew more about the Bible than we do? No, we are not against the people who are being deceived by her teachings. Catholic people believe they're doing an excellent thing by praying to Miriam, the mother of God; but are being deceived by the Institution itself (Rev. 17:5-18).

Do you really think Miriam of the Bible expected generations of people to pray to her? Where in the Bible does anyone pray to a dead human woman? Would Catholics be overjoyed to find that living for Messiah does not require all that liturgy, idolatry, procession confusion and guilt? Here is a gentle message for my Catholic friends. After waiting up to a year in the normal Jewish courtship and then nine more months of pregnancy, I would hope Miriam and Joseph would have behaved like honeymooners! Surely Miriam did enjoy her God invented and God approved marital relations, just as much as the rest of us.

Is the Cross a Christian Symbol?

Here's what I thought I knew: The cross is a holy symbol. We have them on our church steeples, on our altars in the churches, on our walls, hanging from our necks and our rear view mirrors.

Here's the elongated elaborated version: A crucifix on the wall of the church reminds Christians of God's act of love and atonement in Christ's sacrifice at Calvary, "the Lamb of God who takes away the sin of the world." The sacred crucifix also reminds Christians of Jesus' victory over sin and death, since it is believed that through His death and resurrection, He conquered death itself.

Here's more to consider: The cross was never a Christian symbol before Yeshua the Messiah was born. The cross was not considered to be a Christian symbol for hundreds of years after Yeshua was nailed to one.

A "crucifix" is a cross with the Lord still nailed to it. Do you think He is honored if you have one of these hanging from your neck? The above elongated elaborated statement is Catholic in origin. With all the fancy talk about what the crucifix means on the walls of our churches, there is total avoidance of it being originally a pagan idol and an instrument of torture and death.

If the cross is a Christian symbol, why does the occult use it so much? If the cross is a Christian symbol, why is it traceable way back to Babylon and Egypt as far back as 2000 BC? Many ancient cultures used crosses or the mystic Tau. The Greek is "stauros," meaning stake. Babylon seems to be the originator from ancient Chaldea. But you can find crosses from Egypt, India, China, Africa, Mexico, Greece, Italy and South American histories; all before Yeshua the Messiah was ever born!

If pagans had never used crosses as idols and then developed them into instruments of torture and death, you never would have thought to wear a cross with diamonds on a necklace.

The cross is a most sacred idol to the big church in Rome. This point in itself should raise suspicion. Constantine supposedly had a vision of a cross, then after a victory in battle, it was made the official symbol of Rome. But it was more than 150 years until the cross made it all the way up to the steeples. In the 6th century, the Church of Rome sanctioned the cross. Believe it or not, at the council of Ephesus, it was decreed that a cross was a "requirement" in every home.

Of course, it is not "considered" to be an idol anymore, because some pope says it is holy. What do you think God's feelings are on this? Does YHVH say, "Well, if it is okay with the pope, then it's okay with Me?" Remember, something can still be an idol, whether you worship, or bow down before it, or not.

But some would argue that a Christian cross is different from all those "other crosses." Is that like saying you have a pot-bellied pig, but he is different from all those "other pigs"? What you "think" a cross means today does not change the fact of it formerly being a pagan idol, or what it really represents.

Do you think any of the disciples would have been inclined to enter a building with a big cross on its steeple, a week before or after Yeshua had been nailed to one? Wouldn't they have thought it was a house of crucifixion rather than a house of God?

What if the disciples were transported to here and now today? Would they want to enter a church with a big cross on it? The cross was a very horrible torture instrument of the day. Nobody at that time would have ever glorified it, wrote a song about it, or made a little wooden one to hang on their neck.

If the Lord had been shot by an assault rifle when He atoned for our sins, I truly believe people would have a little "M-16" hanging from their necklace. They would probably have an "M-60" machine gun on every steeple too; and the longer the belt of bullets, the "holier" the people would feel.

There is a difference between believing in what was accomplished on the cross and by "Whom;" and wearing one on your necklace. Should we have one constantly displayed like a good luck charm or amulet? Long ago, the Israelites lost sight of the original purpose and began to worship and burn incense to Nehushtan; and because of the misuse it had to be destroyed (2 Kings 18:4).

If nobody can tell you are a believer by your speech, actions, love and life you live; then no amount of hardware around your neck, on your dash, on your wall, or on your steeple will convince them either.

Have you ever slowly read and considered the words in the hymn, "Old Rugged Cross"? There is virtually no glory given to the Lord in the whole song. It concentrates on and glorifies the item, rather than the Deity, throughout the verses. The Bible does not say the cross was rugged, or that it was on a hill, or that it was far away!

Not only was the Lord displeased with idols, to bring them into our house would be forbidden (Deut. 7:25, 26). What were you supposed to do? Burn them with fire (Deut. 7:5). Even so much as enquiring how other people worshiped their gods was forbidden, as well as doing likewise (Deut. 12:30, 31). The punishment for doing so is found in (Deut. 17:2-5). Oh, and what was that second (Exod. 20:4, 5) commandment again? You shall not make any graven images. C'mon now, how stupid are we? There is absolutely no difference between the New Testament view (1 John 5:21) and the Old Testament view about idols. You shall not do so unto the Lord (Deut. 12:4).

Did Mary have other Children after Yeshua?

Here's what I thought I knew: Mary did have other children after Yeshua. Mary did not have other children after Yeshua. Which is it? Can we be sure?

Here's more to consider: When speaking of the brother, or brothers and sisters of Messiah; the Greek word used is (adelphos), which means: "of the same womb, brother, relative." It does say that Yeshua was the "firstborn," not the second or third born (Luke 2:7).

If this is not a satisfactory explanation, there are several other possibilities I've heard offered on this subject.

Mary did not have other children. The brothers and sisters mentioned in the Bible could be Yeshua's cousins. The cousins could have been Joseph's brother's children, who Joseph would have taken on if his brother died. But, they still would have been referred to as brothers and sisters. Or, what if Joseph had children with his brother's widow also?

Mary did not have other children. The brothers and sisters mentioned in the Bible could have been Joseph's children from a previous marriage. In this case, the brothers and sisters would have been blood relation to the family, not just cousins.

The last possibility is any combination of the above. Mary had children and Joseph left behind children from a previous marriage or a brother who had died. If Joseph died and Joseph's brother took on Mary and hers, it would also make the cousins be called their brothers and sisters.

Does anybody today know the answer? With what little the Bible says on the matter, can we be absolutely sure?

CHAPTER FIVE

The Pre-Tribulation Rapture

Here's what I thought I knew: In our future there is going to be a seven year tribulation period with Anti-Christ ruling the earth. The believers (who have been raptured out of the earth) are spending those seven years in heaven at the marriage supper of the Lamb.

Here's a lot more to consider: There is not one verse that mentions a "seven year tribulation period." There is not one verse stating believers will be raptured away seven years before His coming. There is not one verse that says some Anti-Christ is going to rule the world for a seven year period. There is not one verse stating non-believers will have seven extra years to repent before the second coming. I believed this pre-tribulation rapture teaching for many years until someone shared with me what I'm about to share with you. I found it quite interesting that neither, Wycliffe, Huss, Luther, Knox, Calvin, Tyndale, Newton, Wesley, Whitfield, Edwards, Finney or Spurgeon believed in a pre-tribulation rapture.

Those that expect a seven year tribulation period say that the first 3 ½ years will be a time of "peace and safety." Wouldn't that only leave 3 ½ years of tribulation? John wrote he was their companion in tribulation. Did John think he was in the tribulation period in his day? (Rev. 1:9) If so; wouldn't that seven years be over by now?

The pre-tribulation rapture hinges upon Daniel's 70th week being yet unfulfilled. Is there any indication the prophetic clock stopped (Dan. 9:24-27) and seven years was to be postponed until some point in "our" future? It also hinges upon one of these verses secretly meaning the Anti-Christ, when it is blatantly obvious they are all specifically about Messiah.

Pre-tribulation thought teaches the world will go through seven terrible years while believers are in heaven enjoying the marriage supper. The book of Revelation indicates the marriage supper is "after" the Lord's second coming and taking place "here" on earth (Rev. 19:17, 18). Where in the Bible does it say that we ever go to heaven, as a destination or abode? It says there will be a new heaven and a new earth. Previous to 1827, try to find any writings of the rapture occurring seven years before His coming. It seems Edward Irving started the teaching. Darby and the Plymouth Brethren kept it alive through the 1800's. Scofield made it well known by including it in his Bible commentaries. Then Ironside, Willmington, Blackstone, DeHaan and numerous others began to spread this teaching further.

Where did the supposed seven year tribulation period and rapture thinking come from anyway? Around 1827, Edward Irving (who is remembered for his sermon "the sinful nature of Christ") spent two years learning Spanish. He wanted to translate a book, "The coming of Christ in majesty and glory" written by a Catholic, Manual Lacuna, under the pen name of Ben Ezra. The book stated that from the coming forth from heaven and before the arrival to earth, the Lord will call His own to Him. Incorrectly using (Dan.9:27) as a proof text, Edward Irving invented this period of time into seven years! It had never been heard of previously. John Darby also had some influence in promoting this teaching.

Edward Irving was kicked out of his church for varying reasons, including heresy. There is a book about Edward Irving called "The Father of the Charismatic movement." Besides being a sad story, it mentions (but doesn't go into detail) his affiliation with the Pre-tribulation rapture origin. Now, officially called "Dispensationalism," many think this is truth and fact. Let's examine this theory and what they teach, point by point, and compare what the Bible actually says.

If nobody knows when He will return and the believers are raptured out seven years before His coming, won't the remaining non-believers left behind on earth have the luxury of counting seven years and know "exactly" when the Lord will return? Did you ever notice, there is not one verse stating there will be seven more years to repent and be saved before His "other" second coming? Do not listen to those who think they are going to be raptured out with the "first load." The "Left Behind" books and movies were written as fiction, and have no merit or validity. This also means people are being deceived into a false sense of security. They believe they will have seven extra years to repent, so they can ignore spiritual matters now. Should we put off spiritual matters until we get a wakeup call that we have less than seven years left to get it right? Does this sound like a Bible concept? Is there a verse that says this? This makes Christians look for some Anti-Christ to come, because they "think" the arrival of Anti-Christ signals the start of the seven year countdown to our blessed Hope, Yeshua's return! How did we start looking for Anti-Christ to come, and how did he get our focus instead of the Lord?

"Come up hither" is a statement made by the angel to John, to show him things to come (Rev. 4:1). This is not symbolic of the rapture. There are two other verses that have the words "come hither" (Rev. 11:12) (Rev. 21:9). Do these verses represent the rapture also? How can you possibly be sure? If the rapture signals the start of the tribulation, why does (1 Cor. 15:52) say at the "last" trumpet"? Doesn't the resurrection (rapture) occur "at" Messiah's coming, (1 Thess. 4:17) when the dead and living rise to meet Him in the air?

Revelation states, there were souls beheaded for their testimony to Yeshua. They had not worshiped the beast or its image and had not received the mark on their foreheads or hands (Rev. 20:4). If the mark of the beast is something that should happen during the tribulation period, isn't that supposed to be "avoided" by their pre-tribulation rapture?

We must remember the book of Revelation is John writing to the seven churches in Turkey concerning events happening in their day (Rev. 1:1, 3) (Rev. 22:10). Back when John was writing this, to voice that Domitian was god gave one the ability to buy and sell in the marketplace. At the time, this was considered to take "the mark of the beast."

93

Let's examine man of sin, Anti-Christ, son of perdition.
If all believers are raptured out before the Anti-Christ comes to power, who will the Anti-Christ persecute for seven years? Paul states plainly, "the day of the Lord (His return) will not come until the man of sin is revealed" (2 Thess. 2:3, 4). Did you know that Judas (John 17:12) was also called the son of perdition? Will the ruler of a False Religion from Rome resemble Judas? Will he pretend to be a believer, yet is not? Martin Luther said the papacy was the Anti-Christ, and in return the papacy said Luther was the Anti-Christ. One of them is probably right!

John is the only New Testament writer to use the word "antichrist," but it is not found in the book of Revelation (or Daniel) at all. It carries a two-fold meaning: "opponent of God" and/or "in place of God/counterfeit," so it very well could be someone or a group subtly representing darkness that you wouldn't really expect. These verses from John do not even give a hint of a seven year rule at the end of the age. In fact, it sounds like he is speaking of something taking place in his day.

You've heard that antichrist is coming, but there are now many antichrists, therefore we know it is the last time (1 John 2:18).

A liar denies that Yeshua is the Messiah. He is antichrist who won't accept Messiah and has not God (1 John 2:22).

It is the spirit of antichrist which you heard is coming and now is already in the world; that does not acknowledge Yeshua came in the flesh and is not from God (1 John 4:3).

A deceiver and antichrist is one who does not confess that Yeshua came in the flesh (2 John 7).

These antichrists were not atheists. They were "professing Christians" who had crept in unaware. They were teaching counterfeit, distorted, false and erroneous doctrines that were deceiving people seductively (Jude 4). Paul elaborates on this topic in his letter to Titus (Titus 1:10-16). Is the man of sin just one man? Or, is he a succession of men in the same position, like the Caesars? The man of sin will have all power, signs and wonders, unrighteous deceit, lack of truth and strong delusion causing lies to be believed (2 Thess. 2:9-12). Nobody has more of these than the big church in Rome. They have statues that bleed and shed tears, also relics that change color for crowds. They have five mile long lines of people waiting to kiss some shroud, idol, relic, statue, man's ring or holy bone. They have voices from crosses and visits from Mary, who they worship as the mother of god. They have statues that move, light their own candles and heal people. They supposedly have had souls appearing from purgatory requesting masses be said for them. They have even made the evening news, flocking from miles around to see Mary's face in the knot of a tree or Jesus' face in a pizza!

Is the pope the "man of sin"? Is the pope the head of the seat of spiritual impurity that continues to rule and reign from Rome? The pope claims to be the head of the church, but we know Yeshua alone is Head of the church (Col. 1:18). If there is to be another False Religion that rules from Rome, won't it have to wipe out what the Catholic Church has established? Then, wouldn't the new False Religion have to repeat the same things the Catholic Church has previously done? Countless scholars, even Catholic scholars from centuries past have associated the papacy with the beast.

Do you remember (Dan. 7:24) the 10 horns? The Roman Empire was divided into ten Gothic tribes or kingdoms. There were Heruli, the Suevi, the Burgundians, the Huns, the Franks, the Ostragoths, the Visigoths, the Vandals, the Lombards and the Anglo-Saxons. Do you remember the little horn (Dan. 7:8) that plucks up or subdues three kingdoms? When the Roman Empire fell, the papacy rose to power, still ruling and reigning from Rome. The papacy overthrew three of the kingdoms; the Heruli in 493, the Vandals in 534 and the Ostragoths in 553.

The little horn wears out the saints of the Most High (Dan. 7:25). Who else is responsible for torturing and killing as many as 50 million Christians and Jews than Rome and the papacy? The city of Bezier was besieged by men from the Pope that killed 60,000 people in 1209.

The estimates are that 100,000 Albigenses were slaughtered in one day. After attending high mass in the morning, the crusaders accomplished this massacre at Lavaur, in 1211.

People were dragged through the streets, hurled from cliffs, and children murdered in front of their powerless parents. 500 women were locked in a barn and set on fire. If any tried to escape out the windows, they were met with points of spears at the massacre of Merindol.

Pope Pius 4th had men, women and children killed with tortures of every imagination in Orange (1562).

In 1572 10,000 Protestants were killed in St. Bartholomew's Day massacre. The French King went to Mass to give thanks that so many heretics (Huguenots) were killed. The Pope rejoiced with the news and ordered coins made to commemorate this "great event."

"The Inquisition of Spain" by Llorente, acknowledges more than 300,000 suffered in Spain alone. Over 30,000 died in flames and millions were slain for their faith throughout Europe.

There were priests, bishops and cardinals who were registered members with the Nazi party. For years the Vatican was heavily involved with smuggling numerous Nazi war criminals to safety in South America, both during and after World War II.

This is only a fraction of the bloody history of the big church in Rome. Don't get mad at me. All of these events happened way before we were born. Just look it up and verify it for yourself. Where are the torture dungeons in Europe? Under Cathedrals!

If the "hinderer or restrainer" is the Holy Spirit, why would Paul use such veiled, secretive speech (2 Thess. 2:6-8) "if" he were referring to the Spirit? Especially, when he mentions the Spirit openly in (verse 13) of the same chapter! Was he implying the restrainer is the "Roman Empire," that will be taken out of the way when the little horn takes its place? Rome could not be down talked in writing or in speech, for risk of treason and death. Paul knew Rome had to take a fall, making way for the little horn (the papacy) to rise to power, still ruling and reigning from Rome. Did they understand from Daniel's prophecy that the little horn taking Rome's place (still ruling from Rome) would be the seat of Spiritual impurity that would devour the whole earth? The replacement (papacy) would be more terrible and ferocious than its predecessor, the Roman Empire. Are Catholic doctrines really that distorted and unbiblical? There is more written about this subject than you can read in your lifetime. Let's condense it enough to consider a few significant observations and comparisons.

Call no man Father on the earth, for you have one Father in heaven (Matt. 23:9). Priests are called father and the pope is even called "the holy father."

A pastor must be the husband of one wife (1 Tim. 3:2). Catholic priests are forbidden to marry. We all know how well that has been working for them. But it isn't widely broadcast that even some popes had wives and children!

We must keep ourselves from idols (1 John 5:21). The Vatican condones and promotes idol worship.

We are supposed to love our enemies (Matt. 5:39, 44). The papacy thought Protestant Christians should be crushed like venomous snakes in the Inquisition.

Don't pray using vain repetitions like heathens (Matt. 6:7). Don't they say the "hail Mary" prayer about 50 times in a row?

Yeshua is the Head of the church (Eph. 5:23). The pope says he is the head of the church.

We should study the Scriptures (Acts 17:11). Pope Pius 4th didn't think the Bible was proper for the people and should be renounced. It is a forbidden book, and Bible students are Satanic. Pope Nicholas 1st and Pope Gregory 7th put a ban on Bible reading. Pope Gregory 9th forbade Bible possession and ordered them entirely wiped out (1229). Pope Innocent 3rd ordered all who read the Bible should be put to death. Possessing or reading the Bible was forbidden according to the Council of Tolouse and the Council of Trent. Pope Pius 7th said the Bible was a pestilence back in 1816. Pope Gregory 16th condemned the Bible and ordered priests to destroy as many as they could find (1844). The Council of Tarragona ruled Bibles should be given to bishops to be burned. Pope Pius 9th thought Bible societies were pests and must be destroyed by all means (1866).

The Council of the Vatican declared the infallibility of the popes in the mid 1800's.

Since the 16th century, the Vatican declares the Virgin Mary absolutely sinless, making her a female god. They even say she was caught up to heaven without dying and crowned queen of heaven. Do you really think Mary wanted millions of people to pray to her? Is praying to a dead human woman found in the Bible?

We only pray to the Lord our God. But, the Vatican promotes praying to dead people (saints) like St. Christopher for protection. Do you really think a saint can protect you?

Is that enough to consider for us to make an educated decision? It's a little hard to believe, huh? Martin Luther also found many more than just these. I cannot help but wonder, after all these generations of documented accusations and bad press, why wouldn't somebody in Rome realize this? Why wouldn't they even attempt to make some changes so they would not look like a Bible adversary or a false church? Or, did they ever really have a choice but to fulfill what God laid out in Bible prophecy? Imagine John, Daniel and Paul alive here today, to witness how the papacy has fulfilled the prophecies about taking the place of the Roman Empire. These men would have so much to say, we would not be able to get a word in edgewise!

The Roman Catholic Church has had 1,500 years to spread her heresies, false doctrines, idolatry and observances around the world. The Protestant movement and Christianity are peppered with some of her erroneous doctrines that they still carry today. Rome has changed the Sabbath from Saturday to Sunday, changed the Ten Commandments, condoned and promoted idolatry. They pray to and worship the dead human woman who bore Messiah and have re-written the identity of YHVH into a trinity. And why is Rome now called our "church forefathers" when they were the ones who tortured and executed so many of our Jewish and Christian church forefathers? No, we are not against the people who are being deceived by her teachings. Catholic people believe they are doing a good job for Mary, but are being deceived by the Institution itself (Rev. 17:5-18).

For centuries Rome is known as the city built on seven hills (Rev. 17:9). These hills are the Viminal Hill, the Aventine Hill, the Esquiline Hill, the Capitoline Hill, the Caelian Hill, the Quirinal Hill and the Palatine Hill. The Vatican is not actually located on one of the "seven hills" of Rome. It is across the Tiber River to the west and was not considered a part of Rome or included inside Rome's walls erected by Emperor Aurelian. The Vatican is built upon a former graveyard, supposedly guarded by the Etruscan goddess of the underworld, Vatika.

What about the "mortal head wound" (Rev. 13:3, 12, 14) delivered to the beast that will be ruling from Rome? Is this reference about the fall of Rome and the rise of the papacy to take its place? For a long time, I thought the Protestant Movement kind of fit the "wound" criteria too. There is another event that might deserve a little consideration. Napoleon wanted to rule the world, but the papacy stood in the way. Napoleon had a general named Berthier, who actually captured pope Pius 6th on 20 Feb., 1798 and took him back to France. The pope was held hostage for a year and a half and died in France on 29 Aug., 1799. The papacy's power was diminished, but not gone totally. Rome's political power was crushed, but they remained the religious power they had grown to be. Then Cardinal Gaspari and Mussolini made a pact on 11 Feb., 1929, making the Vatican an independent state and the pope was a king again. The San Francisco Chronicle front page account actually read, "Mussolini and Gaspari sign historic pact, Heal wound of many years." Do any of these fit the Scripture?

The falling away (2 Thess. 2:3) or apostasy means to forsake one's religion or faith, a rebellion against or departure from faith, religion, established truth or principles. To try to read the rapture into the "apostasy" totally goes against the Greek and English meanings. There was evidence in Paul's day of the mystery of iniquity already at work (2 Thess. 2:7). Some were distorting the truth (Acts 20:29, 30). There will be some who will abandon the true faith (1 Tim. 4:1-5). Some will introduce destructive heresies and erroneous doctrines (2 Pet. 2:1-3). Peter mentions ignorant and unstable people who distorted what Paul wrote, as well as the Scriptures (2 Pet. 3:15-17). None of these cases involved people leaving the church. They were church going members who were advocating erroneous doctrines and distorting established truths within the church.

Have you noticed the "fig tree" (Matt. 24:32) (Mark 13:28) does not symbolize the nation of Israel? The parallel account in Luke says; Behold the fig tree and "all the trees" (Luke 21:29, 30). Symbolically this would have to include "all the nations." This implies the Lord was simply speaking of being aware of the signs taking place around them. For the fig tree to represent Israel blooming since 1948, it would have to also include "all the trees" (nations) blooming for the sign to be complete, wouldn't it? Israel is symbolized by the "olive tree" in other verses (Jer. 11:16) (Hos. 14:6) (Rom. 11:17, 24).

Six Greek words: heko (Rev. 2:25); erchomai (Luke 19:13); phaneroo (1 John 3:2); epiphaneia (1 Tim. 6:14); apokalupsis (1 Pet. 1:7); and parousia (James 5:7) are used interchangeably about the one event–Yeshua's return. There are numerous passages using each of the previous six words interchangeably about the second coming. I provided just one verse for each word. Most people think apocalypse (apokalupsis, apokalupto) means some catastrophic cataclysmic event. If you look in your concordance, it simply means and is only used for the revealing, appearing, and manifestation of the Lord's second coming. That event may be accompanied by some unusual occurrences, but apocalypse means "His revealing."

Yeshua shall appear to those who look for Him to return a

second time (Heb. 9:28). They were waiting and looking for, the appearing (Titus 2:13) (I Thess. 5:23) of our great Saviour. Don't the Gospel accounts plainly state, "when" Yeshua is seen coming in the clouds, (Matt. 24:30, 31) (Mark 13:26, 27) "then" His angels will gather His elect?

He said, "Endure to the end" (Matt. 24:13) (Mark 13:13). How can this be accomplished if we are taken out seven years before the end? Yeshua stated, "I will come again and receive you unto Myself" (John 14:3). Plainly, it is when Yeshua returns that He receives us unto Himself, and not seven years earlier. Why are the brethren exhorted to be patient unto the coming of the Lord, if their real hope was the rapture seven years earlier?

He that shall come, "will come" (James 5:1) (Heb. 10:36, 37). Paul writes (1 Cor. 1:7) that we are waiting for the "coming" of our Lord. Paul writes in another letter that the living and remaining believers will not precede the dead "at His coming" (1 Thess. 4:15). Yeshua said to be ready for the "coming" of the Son (Matt. 24:44).

Here's a thought. "If" the believers had been with the Lord in heaven for seven years, how much of a surprise would the "second coming" be? Who would be caught unaware, if all the believers He is coming for; were raptured out and had been with Him for the past seven years? Yeshua said, "The wheat and the tares will grow together until the harvest" (Matt. 13:24-30). He explained who sows the wheat and the tares, and the harvest is the close of the age (Matt. 13:37-39). He specifically states, the tares first are gathered, then the wheat will be gathered (Matt. 13:30).

He told us all the fish are separated at the end of the world (Matt. 13:47-50). "All people will be called from their graves" (John 5:28, 29). Paul looked forward to resurrection at His coming, not a point seven years earlier (1 Cor. 15:23). As in the days of Noah, there was buying, selling, marrying, and business as usual, then one day the flood came (Matt. 24:37-39). The Lord's return could be at any time, like a whistle blowing, "Party's over, everybody out of the pool!"

Most people don't bother reading the rest of the verse, "the day of the Lord will come as a thief in the night" (2 Pet. 3:10). First of all, Peter is speaking of the Lord coming "unexpectedly" as a thief would, and not about the Lord sneaking in and out undetected. The rest of the verse states, there will be a great noise, fervent heat and the elements and heavens melting and dissolving with fire." This is hardly a secret, sneaky, un-noticed event, is it? (Rev. 16:15 is pre-return also, and we're still here!)

What prophecy experts sometimes jokingly referred to as "the yo-yo effect" (believers being caught up to meet the Lord in the air and returning with Him to earth), is exactly what the word "meet" means in the original Greek. The word "meet" (apantesis) may be the most important indication "when" the resurrection will really take place (1 Thess. 4:17). You never heard the tribulation teachers talk about this before, have you? Prophecy preachers elaborate on the Greek meaning of a word and they obviously know about this one too, but conveniently avoid mentioning the Greek meaning of the word "meet."

Apantesis is the custom of going to "meet" those traveling to visit you (especially royalty) and escorting them to their destination. The men of Rome "apanteo'd" as far as Appii Forum, which was about 40 miles (Acts 28:15). This gave them more time (while traveling) to spend with Paul, than those waiting for his arrival. The same word is used in the parable of ten virgins who went to "meet" (apanteo) the bridegroom and returned with Him (Matt. 25:1, 6).

There will be those who "are not" in the book of life, who worship the beast; and there will be the saints who "are" in the book of life, with whom the beast makes war (Rev. 13:7, 8). How can the beast make war with the saints if they were "supposed" to be gone in the rapture?

According to the "6 day theory" there has been 2,000 years from Adam to the flood, 2,000 years from the flood to Yeshua and 2,000 years from Yeshua to now. Simply by adding up the ages given in Genesis, there may have been only 1,656 years from Adam to the flood. This puts the "6 day theory" more than two centuries short of the needed 6,000 years to uphold that view. The Jewish calendar is on 5770 or (2009). Have you read the verses they use to substantiate this "6 day theory"? Peter states that a day "with" the Lord is like a thousand years and a thousand years is like a day (2 Peter 3:8). Are we "with" the Lord now? Is this a magic formula for us to calculate when the Lord will return?

There is another verse that is similar (Psalms 90:4). "A thousand years in God's sight are as yesterday when it is past and as a watch in the night." As I recall, the night watch was split into several shifts. Is a thousand years like a "shift" of a night watch? The entire night watch does not even equal a whole day and is still only half of a day. Were these verses intended to be a formula for us to determine when the Lord will return, or simply a reminder how God is not restricted by time?

What about the millennium time period? Revelation 20 is the only chapter in the entire Bible to mention the 1,000 years or millennium. If we look closely, the books are opened after a universal resurrection, with a separation and universal judgment of good and bad alike, immediately following the millennium (verses 11-15). Why would there still be a beast after He returns (verse 4), and a choice to take its mark? This agrees completely with the Lord's descriptions in the gospels about the separation of the good and bad fish, wheat and tares, sheep and goats after He returns. It appears to be obvious; the spiritual Kingdom ushered in by Messiah is one and the same as the millennium. This millennium can only be the time period between the incarnation and the second coming, because judgment for everyone follows the event of His return.

Many people are anticipating a charismatic world leader to implement a bar-code or computer chip in everybody's right hand or forehead for identification purposes, and for buying and selling (Rev. 13:16-18). Is this symbolism simply, who you believe in (forehead) and who you serve (right hand)? Or is this a statement from John warning the seven churches in Turkey not to call Domitian god or "take the mark of the Beast" to buy and sell "back in their day"?

The 144,000 are said to have the seal of God upon their foreheads (Rev. 7:3, 14:1). There are those who have the seal of God upon their foreheads and there are the beast worshipers who have the mark upon their forehead or hand (Rev. 14:9). The believers are said to have His name on their foreheads (Rev. 22:4). Even the description, "Babylon the great, mother of harlots and of earth's abominations" is on the whore's forehead (Rev. 17:5). Is everybody going to have stuff on their foreheads in the near future?

Did you know the "abomination of desolation" (Matt. 24:15) (Mark 13:14) has already happened? How many times does this prediction need to be fulfilled? It was 70 AD when Titus destroyed Jerusalem. For the Anti-Christ to be able to destroy the Temple, it would have to be rebuilt for a third time to be destroyed again, right? Why would Anti-Christ want to rule and reign from a desolated Temple with one stone not upon another? Many people only use Matthews' statement. But if we look at what Luke's parallel account says, "When you see Jerusalem surrounded by armies, flee without running to get your coat" (Luke 21:20). It is said that "not even one Christian perished" in the destruction of Jerusalem. Why? Because they understood what the Lord had meant by this.

Why do Matthew, Mark and Luke speak of upcoming destruction, abomination of desolation and one stone not left upon another, but John doesn't mention it? They wrote their accounts before the destruction of Jerusalem in 70 AD; John wrote his account after. The destruction was past history and there was no more need to put out the warning.

What about Ezekiel chapters 38 and 39?

Do Ezekiel chapters 38 and 39 describe an ancient battle or a future war? Even if the Hebrew word for "arrow" and "missile" are the same, how many modern missiles have you seen launched by a wooden bow? Or could be burned for cooking (Ezek. 39:3, 9, 10) or heat? The shields, bucklers, hand staves and spears are also included in the burnable weapons of war. Are these modern weapons of war to be burned for seven years? Is wood in the field and the forest the major source of fuel for cooking and heat nowadays? It says that all come on horseback (Ezek. 38:4, 15). Doesn't this describe primitive transportation?

It says they all are handling swords and clothed with armor, a great company with bucklers and shields (Ezek. 38:4, 5). Doesn't this describe primitive weapons?

It says, "Gold, silver, cattle and goods are the spoils of war" (Ezek. 38:12, 13). How many current battles are fought where "cattle" are the main spoils of war? Israel will be dwelling "safely and at rest" in villages without walls (Ezek. 38:11). The walls about the city used to serve as an important factor for defense. Are walls important in war today? Has Israel been dwelling "safely and at rest" with or without walls since 1948?

Sometimes we are told the "scattered among the nations" verses from (Ezek. 12:10-15) are applied to Israel re-gathering to become a nation again in 1948. Surely Ezekiel was talking about the seventy year captivity in Babylon, as in (Jer. 29:10-14) and the return to Israel afterwards; not about something in our future. Although this fulfilled prophecy of a surrounding nation attacking and capturing Israel could happen again; would that be what Ezekiel was actually predicting in his day?

Have you ever looked up the meaning of "Gog"? How about the root word from which it is derived? Believe it or not, it seems the root and meaning remain completely unknown. It could be as simple as "the enemy of God's people." Did you notice Gog is a prince (Ezek. 38:1-3, 39:1) or chief ruler in one place? But in another place, Gog is called a nation (Rev. 20:8).

Did you notice Gog is from the land (Ezek. 38:2) of Magog? But in another place, Gog and Magog are both nations from the four corners of the earth, that number like sand on the seashore (Rev. 20:8). Did you notice Gog (a prince) comes against Israel (Ezek. 38, 39) with others from different countries located around Israel? But in another place, Gog and Magog are described as nations in all the earth (Rev. 20:8). Did you notice

Gog's army is defeated in Israel, and they burn (Ezek. 39:9) the weapons for seven years? But in another place, Gog and Magog are burned up with fire from heaven (Rev. 20:9). Wouldn't wooden weapons also be burned up immediately by fire from heaven? If this is the final battle at the end of time, would seven more years to burn the weapons be important?

Josephus records Noah's grandson Magog (through Japheth) who named his nation "the Magogites," after his own name, but Greeks called them Scythians. There is an area in eastern Iran (Balochistan) also called Sakastan, which means "home of the Scythians" (or Magogites). Another grandson, Gomer, named his people the Gomerites, who settled in the NE area just above the Mediterranean Sea, and whom the Greeks call Galatians (Galls) (Antiquities of the Jews book 1, 6:1). This is at least 1,000 miles away from Germany!

Another wild claim is "Russia" coming down from the north (Ezek. 38:3). The word "rosh" is used over 600 times in Scripture. It simply means "chief or head" and not Russia. Would Israel have been aware that Russia even existed, thousands of miles north of them?

We are also told that Meshech means "Moscow" and Tubal means "Tobolsk." Moscow is a Finnish name and is first mentioned in ancient documents in 1147 AD. Tobolsk was founded in 1587 AD. Though similar in sound, there is no further association. Yes, Germany and Gomer both start with "G" and so does guessing. Iowa and India both start with "I" and so does imagination. Alaska and Antarctica start with an "A" but they are not the same place.

The word translated 'latter' in (Ezek. 38:8, 16) means "future or later on" (Strong's Concordance #319). Ezekiel spoke of what was future to his period in time, not necessarily our point in time. For what purpose would Ezekiel tell Israelites in 700 BC about a war supposedly years in "our" future? Nobody seems to realize that some of the invading tribes were located to the south of Israel. The northern tribes were no further north than the Black Sea. Some of these tribes may have been regions of

106

Turkey. Though not officially recorded, wouldn't (Ezek. 38, 39) have likely been fulfilled about 400 years later, when Antiochus Epiphanes attacked and was defeated? Why do we try to apply every prophecy from history past, to us and our future today?

Some folks try to include verses from Zechariah to add to the Pre-tribulation Rapture Theory, saying this is about the 1,000 year millennium. Why would Zechariah be telling Israelites about things to happen 2,500 years in their future? What would that accomplish for Israel, and how would that benefit them in their day? The context of the book of Zechariah is the time frame before Messiah, because it ends with the offering of sacrifices (Zech. 14:21). The necessity of offering sacrifices ended with the final sacrifice, Messiah. Why would animal sacrifices be expected after His return?

Perhaps the greatest flaw in the Pre-tribulation Rapture Theory, is the attempt to substantiate it with (Dan. 9:24-27). Notice that the 70 weeks or 490 years determined, are upon the Jews and upon their holy city, Jerusalem (Verse 24). Heptad is a plural word, but is used with a singular verb and is more properly translated, "Seventy weeks is determined," describing the 70 weeks as one unit. Wasn't this whole prophecy given to the Jewish people by a Jewish prophet about their Jewish Messiah?

How can we go back 2,500 years and take part of a sentence completely out of context, change the meaning and say that it is meant for our future? We have a verse that is talking about Messiah, then Abra Cadabra all of a sudden, half of the verse is about an Anti-Christ, some 2,000 years in the future from the time frame (Verse 27) of the verse! This is twisted thinking. Without any indication, why would Daniel secretly be telling Israel about some Anti-Christ 2,500 years in their future, inserted into the middle of a Messianic prophecy? Wouldn't they say, huh? The 490 years was no secret. They knew when Artaxerxes Longimanus (458 BC) decreed and funded Jerusalem's rebuild (Ezra 7:11-26), likely starting the 490 year count. This would place Messiah's birth about (5 BC), because we know King Herod died around the full eclipse in Jan. (1 BC). To try to start the 490 years some 13 years later; with the same

Artaxerxes (445 BC) telling Nehemiah (Neh. 2:6-8) to rebuild the walls, would put Messiah's birth around (8 AD). Israel knew Daniel's prophecy and expected Messiah's arrival. Even the chief priests told Herod where He was to be born (Matt. 2:4, 5).

Side note: Artaxerxes Longimanus was reputed to have one or both arms so long, he could touch his knees or below when standing! (Library of Biblical Literature 1856, Vol. 4) (Critical and Popular Bible Encyclopedia 1901, Vol. 1, page 162)

If 69 weeks (483 years) lead up to Messiah's arrival and He gets cut off (crucified) after 3 ½ years of ministry; isn't the week He gets cut off in...the 70th week? Since Messiah is the final sacrifice, He caused the sacrifice (oblation) to cease. Did you notice the 490 years is foretold as seven weeks and 62 weeks and one week? Nobody ever tries to put a 2,000 year gap in between the seven weeks and the 62 weeks, do they?

To put the 70th week some 2,000 years in the future is like putting bubblegum at the 35th inch of a yardstick, so it will measure whatever you want it to. This would also completely eliminate the prophecy and the only verse that accurately predicts the arrival of Messiah at year 483 of the 490; and the death of Messiah after 3 ½ years of ministry. And, if Messiah had fulfilled 486 ½ years of this prophecy before He was crucified, wouldn't there only be 3 ½ years left? After the cross; the Gospel went only to Israel first, and then later the Gentiles were included. Remember when Peter delivered the first salvation message (Acts 10) to the Gentiles? That would be 3 ½ years after the cross, marking the end of the 490 years and Israel's exclusivity to God. Why would anyone try to take this seven year period about Messiah (from around 25-35 AD) and postpone it for our future, with Anti-Christ now being the focus?

Did you notice (Dan. 9:24-27) does not even mention the word "Anti-Christ"? The "he" that starts (verse 27) is a pronoun and a continuation of the sentence in (verse 26), in which the subject noun is the Messiah. How can we insert Anti-Christ into a Messianic prophecy? Even the time frame is a couple thousand years off. That is just like saying (Isa. 9:6) is about Messiah, except the name "Prince of peace," which jumps forward 2,000 years in time and only applies to Anti-Christ! The Hebrew word for "prince" who is to come (Dan. 9:26) simply means "leader." Dan. 9:27 never states, makes a seven year peace treaty. Verse 27 never states, breaks a seven year peace treaty. Verse 27 never states, the temple has to be rebuilt for a third time. Verse 27 never states, animal sacrifices will begin again.

Yeshua prayed we would not be taken out of the world, but be kept from the evil (John 17:15). Noah and Lot were not taken out, but kept through the judgment.

Many people are expecting 144,000 Jewish "Billy Grahams" to start preaching the biggest revival of all time (Rev. 7:4). Does Scripture really predict a big revival or a great apostasy before He returns? Did you notice that the 144,000 are the first fruits? (Rev. 14:3, 4) These are 12,000 Jews from each of the 12 tribes of Israel, and not to be confused with the group that no man could number. Is this a symbolic number for the first Jewish believers in Messiah, whose numbers have surely increased since then? Doesn't James refer to the first Jewish converts from the 12 tribes (James 1:1, 18) to the new covenant and Messiah as "first fruits"? If the Ruach/Holy Spirit is supposedly raptured out with the church, how could the greatest revival of all time be possible? Anyway, if the 144,000 Jewish believers appear at the end this age, won't they be the "last fruits"?

Is the New Jerusalem a literal city; or a symbolic description of the glorified, purified church? Will this physical city rest here on earth or maybe hang like a chandelier in the sky? If it is to hang in the sky, why would it need foundations and walls? If it is a 1,500 mile cube in shape; that is about 7,900,000 feet high! (Remember the Holy of Holies was also a perfect cube in shape 1 Kings 6:20). How much protection do 216 foot walls and gates of pearls provide for a city that size? Wouldn't the city reach into outer space? If only believers are in this New Jerusalem; why would walls even be necessary for protection?

The angel said to John, "Come hither, I will show thee the Bride, the Lamb's Wife. And he showed me that great city, the holy

Jerusalem" (Rev. 21:9, 10). If you look closely, the description of the city's gems are the same 12 gems that were in the Levite priests' breastplate. Streets of gold imply purity. The names of the 12 tribes of Israel are on the gates. The wall had foundations with the names of the 12 apostles. This describes all the Old and New Testament believers as a royal priesthood, the new habitation of the Lord, the New Jerusalem. Why wouldn't the Old Testament righteous be included with the New Testament believers in one body, for the Lord to present to Himself a pure bride, the wife of the Lamb? This is what Paul had to say about one new body of believers (Eph. 2:12-16, 20) (Eph. 3:6, 5:27).

Some are expecting Elijah to arrive at some point in our future (Mal. 4:5, 6). Yeshua said, (Matt. 11:13-15) and (Matt. 17:11-13); and Zacharias (Luke 1:17) said that John the Baptist specifically was the Elijah that was to come. Some expect Elijah and Enoch, Elijah and Moses, or John and Daniel to come as the Two Witnesses. Did you notice the passage in Revelation never identifies (Rev. 11:3-13) the Two Witnesses?

Isn't it suspicious the Pre-tribulation Rapture Theory hinges on there being "two" second comings that are seven years apart? There would also have to be two raptures, one at the beginning of the seven years and a second rapture at the end of the seven years. And why do they teach there will be two Judgment Days that are 1,000 years apart? When it is plainly taught the wicked and the saved will be there at the same time, when the books are opened. They say there will be two destructions by fire, one at His coming and another after a supposed 1,000 years. Wouldn't anyone that could be saved during the supposed seven years of tribulation, obviously miss out on the Marriage Supper that is supposed to take place in heaven for those seven years? So, if you still expect you will be raptured to heaven and luckily avoid a seven year tribulation, don't stop flossing.

And why do they think animal sacrifices will be reinstituted in a "future" millennium? That's religion in reverse. Wouldn't the holes in His hands, feet and side be enough of a reminder of what He sacrificed? Ultimately, Christians are being deceived

110

to look for Anti-Christ to arrive, because they "think" that event will start the seven year countdown to our blessed Hope, Yeshua's return. What if the false worship system from Rome has been here for centuries and we don't even recognize it?

I think we can spend an unhealthy amount of time trying to predict the time of His return. We should be ready all the time, because He could come back anytime. Shouldn't we be proclaiming who He is, what He did, and what it means to any with ears to hear? We should keep an educated watchful eye on Israel, Jerusalem, Islam and whatever may come from Rome. If you want a Jewish sign; what about the eclipses due on both Passover and Sukkot, in the upcoming years of 2014 and 2015?

What does it all boil down to? All the dead will be resurrected for Judgment day. The dead and living believers will rise at His coming into incorruptible bodies and will meet (apanteo) the Lord in the air; then finish the journey with Him back to the earth for rewards and Judgment Day of all good and bad beings alike. This should be followed by the new heavens and new earth or eternity. Isn't being ready much more important than wasting hours trying to pinpoint the exact time frame?

The Day that No Man Knows

Yom Teruah or Rosh HaShanah is the Feast Day that is actually two days (the day that no man knows). Why two days? With 29.5 days counted from one new moon to the next, no one could be sure if the new moon would begin on the 29th or the 30th day of the month; so to be sure, they counted both.

Rosh HaShanah is the first day of a period called the "Ten Days of Awe," which ends with Yom Kippur (Day of Atonement). No man knows exactly when it will begin, due to the fact that the new moon would not be officially sanctified until two witnesses would see the new moon, and attest to it before the Sanhedrin in the Temple. This sanctification could happen at any time during either of the two days, depending on when the witnesses came and gave their report. Your research on this feast will reveal that the Temple doors were only open for a short period of time. It was possible to miss out on the feast if someone failed to make it to the Temple before the doors were shut, and no man could get in.

They had to be earnestly watchful for the shofar to sound during the day, when two were working in the fields, or grinding at the mill (Matt. 24:40-44). The person who was alert and listening would be "taken" by the signal of the trumpet sound, and run for the Temple. The person who was not aware, or paying close attention, would be "left" in the field or grinding at the mill.

If the shofar were to sound at night, they were to be prepared by having their lamps filled with oil; so they could find their way to the Temple in the dark, if necessary. This Feast of Trumpets typology also applies to the ten virgins, of which five were wise and ready for the trumpet sound. The other five were foolish and not prepared for the call, and the resulting shut doors left them out of the feast (Matt. 25:1-13).

Paul likened the Lord to a "thief in the night," who would come at an hour "that no man knows." Those, who were not ready and watching earnestly, could expect sudden destruction to come upon them (1 Thess. 5:2-8).

This "thief in the night" metaphor comes from when the High Priest would make his unscheduled rounds each night to make sure the other priests were doing their duties, one of which was keeping the fire burning on the brazen altar (Lev. 6:13). Because the High Priest usually arrived at an hour they were least expecting him; he was coined, the "thief in the night."

The priests were also commanded not to consume alcohol while serving in the Temple, which would make them drunken, inattentive and sleepy (Lev. 10:9). If a priest were to fall asleep and let the fire go out, it could bring judgment upon Israel.

If the High Priest were to find someone asleep on duty, and not properly tending to the fire on the brazen altar; he might scoop up some coals from the altar with a shovel, and dump them on the sleeping priest's garment. The sleeping priest would wake up to the smell of hot burning coals and his garment on fire. He would strip off his clothes quickly to avoid being burned. When the other priests saw him without his garment, he would be naked and ashamed, because everybody knew he had been caught sleeping on the job.

This is also evident when the Lord warns, "Behold, I come as a thief. Blessed is he that watches and keeps his garments, lest he walk naked and they see his shame" (Rev. 16:15).

The overall lesson in these examples is clear. A diligent awareness and watchfulness of our high calling will be rewarded; and a continued unawareness and indifference to the things of God will catch some unprepared, and be to their ultimate detriment.

Sun darkened, Blood Moon and Falling Stars

Here's what I thought I knew: At some point in our future we can expect to see the stars falling, the sun becoming black and the moon becoming as blood.

Here's more to consider: There are about half a dozen places in Scripture where these terms are used. Either they are literal events or simply Hebrew symbolic prophetic rhetoric.

The destruction of Babylon by the Medes; "For the stars of heaven and the constellations thereof shall not give their light; the sun shall be darkened in his going forth and the moon shall not cause her light to shine" (Isa. 13:10).

The downfall of Edom; "And all the host of heaven shall be dissolved, the heavens shall be rolled together as a scroll and all their host shall fall down..." (Isa. 34:4).
The Lord's judgment upon Egypt; "also the day shall be

darkened...a cloud shall cover her..." (Ezek. 30:18).

The Lord's judgment against Pharaoh, king of Egypt; "And when I shall put thee out, I will cover the heaven, and make the stars thereof dark; I will cover the sun with a cloud and the moon shall not give her light. All the bright lights of heaven will I make dark over thee and set darkness upon thy land, says the Lord God" (Ezek. 32:7, 8).

God's judgment against Jerusalem; "The earth shall quake before them, the heavens shall tremble, the sun and the moon shall be dark and the stars shall withdraw their shining..." (Joel 2:10).

God's judgment against Jerusalem; "The sun shall be turned into darkness and the moon into blood before the great and the terrible day of the Lord" (Joel 2:31).

All these prophecies were written by Jewish prophets to the people of Israel about something concerning them in their future. Why would Old Testament prophets warn the people of Israel about something 2,500 years in their future? Since each of these events has already been fulfilled; there would be nothing in these prophecies that has to do with "our" future.

Jewish prophets wrote these prophecies to Jewish people predicting calamity relative to their point in time. These events are now fulfilled history and past occurrences. History has no record in any of these instances where the heavens rolled up like a scroll, the host of heaven going dark, stars falling, the sun ceasing to give its light, the heavens trembling or the moon turning to blood.

Go outside and look up. Since the sun, moon and stars are still lit and in their places, it obviously has not happened yet. When it happens in our future, it will likely be for the first time. This prophetic rhetoric and figures of speech were predictions of impending doom. These terms were used several times by the prophets to foretell coming judgment, downfall or destruction. They were not solely predicting astronomical events.

114

Absent from the Body, Present with the Lord?

Here's what I thought I knew: As soon as you close your eyes in this human body, you immediately go to heaven and into the Lord's waiting arms or into His presence. Therefore, the moment you are absent from this body, you are immediately present in heaven with the Lord.

Here's more to consider: This is a very commonly used consolation statement for those who are grieving over the loss of a loved one. It's a nice thought, but is it true? Everybody wants to go to heaven, yet nobody wants to die! But, where in the Bible is heaven ever given as the destination of the dead? The idea that man has a conscious state after death comes from Greek and Roman mythology and not from the Bible.

What about Sheol, hades and the grave? It is appointed unto man to live once, die and then stand judgment. Where does the Bible say we get to wait for resurrection and Judgment Day in heaven, or in the presence of the Lord? (Job 7:9, 10) Some people think "hell" is a fiery place of torment and punishment, with the devil and his demons making life miserable for its inhabitants. They mistakenly associate the Judgment Day "lake of fire" with the word "hell."

Hell is translated from the Greek word "hades" (meaning place of the dead, or the grave). Hades has nothing to do with Judgment day, or what any good or bad person did in their life to get there, except die. This means Adam and Eve, my mom and dad, Peter, Paul, Mary, king David, Elijah, Abraham, Isaiah and all others are still in the grave awaiting resurrection at the Lord's second coming; as well as the unsaved in their graves awaiting the same resurrection for Judgment day.

Here are a few verses about the grave: (Job 14:10-12; 17:13-16). For in death there is no remembrance of thee (Ps. 6:5). As one dies, so dies the other (Ps. 49:12). The people and the animals, both have the same breath/Ruach of life (Job 27:3) and they both die (Eccl. 3:19-22). I will ransom them from the power of the grave and from death (Hos. 13:14). Also see the verses in (Job 34:14, 15) (Ps. 115:17, 146:4) (Eccl. 9:10).

People will try to use what the Lord told the thief on the cross as proof for immediate presence in heaven upon death. The Lord certainly would not contradict any teaching already established in His Scripture. (See "Thief on the Cross")

Paul looked forward to being resurrected "at" His coming and receiving his immortal body (1 Cor. 15:51-55). Why would Paul look forward to resurrection at Yeshua's second coming if he thought he would go to heaven as soon as he died? Why would all the New Testament writers be looking forward to the resurrection and second coming, if they knew their real hope was to be in His presence as soon as they died?

Have you heard people use the catch phrase (2 Cor. 5:1-10) "absent from the body, present with the Lord"? Does anybody ever bother to read the rest of the verses? Paul obviously did not think upon death we would go immediately to the Lord, nor was he inferring that when writing to the Corinthians.

While still in his mortal body, Paul's desire for his immortal body and to be present with the Lord was associated with Judgment Day and expected to take place at the Lord's coming (Verse 10). We must notice in his second letter to the Corinthians, Paul did not specify "when" he expected to receive his immortal body and be present with the Lord (at His coming) as he did in his first letter (1 Cor. 15:22, 23).

Paul specifically instructed the Thessalonians about the dead believers who slept in the grave. They still have the same hope of resurrection as we who are living (1 Thess. 4:13-18). The dead will rise first, and then we which are alive and remain will be caught up with them (Verse 16, 17). Paul did not give them the impression that the dead believers had gone ahead of the remaining living believers into the Lord's presence. Paul would never teach the Corinthians one thing, and then teach the

Thessalonians something completely different.

When the Lord told Martha that her brother would rise and live again, she obviously understood that Lazarus and all believers would live again, resurrected on the Last Day (John 11:23, 24). Nobody thought Lazarus went anywhere else but the grave.

Peter even said that King David was dead, buried and still in the grave on the day of Shavuot (Pentecost); and he did not ascend into the heavens (Acts 2:29, 34).

If all the dead believers have been in the Lord's presence since they died; what purpose would it serve for the Lord to pop them back into the grave, just to resurrect them right back out of the grave to be in His presence once again?

There will be a time when "all" the dead will come out of their graves, some to rewards and some to judgment (John 5:28, 29). If our life is what will be judged; this makes every moment even more important and each breath more special and precious, doesn't it? Daniel speaks of when all will come out of the dust, some to life and some to shame (Dan. 12:2). Hebrews Chapter 11 considers all the past souls as "dead in faith."

What if the last thing we remember is our last breath in this body and the next thing we know, we are rising to meet Him in the clouds; totally unaware of the elapsed time from death to resurrection?

We admit this is a gray area, but there is not a shred of evidence that implies we would maintain a conscious state, or go immediately to the presence of the Lord when we die. Bible references do not separate the soul/identity from the body. It is the Ruach (breath/life force) that returns to the Lord.

Rather than attempt to predict what actually happens when we die; isn't it more important for us to concentrate on and honor Him by living a proper Godly life, while we are still alive?

The Parable of the Rich Man and Lazarus

Here's what I thought I knew: The lesson of this parable is about the evil of riches and the blessing of poverty. Sometimes this parable is used to show that we go to a glorious place as soon as we die while the unsaved go to a place of punishment and torment (Luke 16:19-31).

Here's more to consider: This parable has nothing to do with money. If the beggar was rewarded for poverty, why would King David write, (Ps. 37:25) he'd never seen the righteous begging bread? This parable says nothing about a location folks are appointed to upon death. If the rich man is in flaming torment, Judgment Day has already occurred, right? How can someone be sent back to the living to warn his five brothers "after" the Lord has already returned? Can we use part of a verse or part of a parable to change what is already written?

Let's take a look at some important points in this parable. The rich man is clothed in purple (royalty) and fine linen (priesthood) (Verse 19). When they both were dead in the grave, the rich man not only recognized Abraham, but called him "father Abraham" (Verses 23, 24). Is there a Hebrew relation to Abraham? If so, would Lazarus represent the Gentiles?

The rich man wanted a dip of a finger to cool his tongue, because of the torment in the "flame" (singular) (Verse 24). The word "torment" does not mean writhing in fire. It means "to be pained or emotional grief." If he was in the eternal lake of fire, a drop on the tongue would provide little or no relief. Is this a reference to the Living Water of the Gospel?

There was a great chasm between them (Verse 26). Did you notice those who "wanted" to go from Abraham to the rich man could not; nor could anyone with the rich man get to Abraham. If this were a picture of heaven and eternal punishment, why would anyone in Abraham's bosom want to go across and join the rich man? Look up the words for "pass" or "cross over" in your Concordance. They are two different words. The first is "diabaino" and the second is "diaperao." The other 8 uses of these Greek words are associated with crossing over a body of water (Matt. 9:1; 14:34) (Mark 5:21; 6:53) (Acts 16:9; 21:2; 27:5) (Heb. 11:29). The chasm is something that could be full of water; yet cannot be "sailed" over (an irreversible decision?). Why would the rich man want "a drop of water," if there was an impassable gulf full of water between them? Could a decision against Messiah (Living Water) be the "gulf" (separation)?

This could be a symbolic reference to the Israelites looking across the Jordan River to the Promised Land the Lord was going to give them (Deut. 12:10). Or, this could be a reference to Moses looking across the Jordon (Deut. 34:4). The rich man (Israel) is looking across the chasm (separation) at the Promised Land (salvation in Messiah).

The rich man begged for Lazarus to be sent to his father's house to warn his five brothers. Abraham replied, they have Moses and the prophets, let the brothers listen to them (Verses 27-29). This strongly implies the rich man is Hebrew. Even though there 12 tribes of Israel named for 12 brothers, the brothers were not all from the same mother. Was this a reference about Judah, who had five brothers?

The rich man told father Abraham, someone returning from the dead would cause his brothers to "repent" (Verse 30). What would the Hebrew brothers be repenting for? Rejecting Messiah? The time frame when the brothers can still repent could only be prior to the second coming. Abraham responds, they will not be convinced, even if someone rises from the dead (Verse 31). Who is the only One who rose from the dead?

The underlying message meant the Jews (rich man) would regret the decision of rejecting Messiah. The Pharisees who were listening (Luke 16:14), who have had nearly complete exclusivity to God, yet looked down on sinners and Gentiles; would see believers in Messiah and realize they had not recognized their own Lord.

119

Thief on the Cross

Here's what I thought I knew: As soon as the thief on the cross died, he went immediately to Paradise that day (Luke 23:43).

Here's more to consider: If this is true, it would conflict with all the other verses in the Bible about death and the grave. The original Greek had no punctuation. Depending on where you place the comma in the verse, it can change the whole meaning!

I tell you, this day you shall be with Me in paradise.
I tell you this day, you shall be with Me in paradise.

The first example conflicts with a great number of verses. The second example is totally congruent with all of Scripture. Did the Lord or the thief ascend directly to Paradise that day? Three days later, the Lord told Mary not to touch (detain) Him because He had not yet ascended (John 20:17). Did the thief get to go to Paradise that day ahead of the Lord? Do not forget, no man has ascended up to heaven, except He that came down from heaven, Yeshua Himself (John 3:13). It is appointed unto man to die once, and after that comes judgment (Heb. 9:27).

The thief had little time that day to live a changed life. He never had a chance to be baptized in Yeshua's name or give some evidence of being filled with the Spirit. The thief recognized, understood and believed the Messiah was nailed beside him. He was repentant and had faith in the One who forgives. This faith alone, qualified the thief for the same expectation of resurrection which we all look forward to, "at" His second coming.

The works of his life got him nailed to a cross. It was his pure faith, belief and understanding he was speaking with the Lord that gave him the same promise at the resurrection that we also seek and desire. There is no verse indicating the thief would be anywhere ahead of anybody else.

CHAPTER SIX

Trinity...The Forbidden Topic

Here's what I thought I knew: There is one God, manifested in three separate, distinct persons. Each person is co-equal, co-powerful, co-eternal and neither is greater or lesser than the other. Their glory is also co-equal. They never argue, and they are always in agreement with each other. Views differ as to the Father sending the Spirit through the Son, or the Father and the Son both send the Spirit. Each person has their own divine function in agreement with the others.

Here's more to consider: The terms "trinity" and "triune" are not found in the Bible. This is a case where a doctrine can sound good, yet fail to be good sound doctrine. Even people who believe God is three persons admit this doctrine is not expressed in any specific form in the Old or New Testaments. We must ask, why this blind allegiance to Constantine?

It seems every time the subject of the trinity comes up; it causes nothing but confusion, anger and division. Are confusion, anger and division proper biblical ideals for us? What about the phrase "views differ" about Who sends the Spirit? After 1,700 years, can't they get their story straight once and for all? And these folks wrote and profess to understand it! The trinity doctrine is Christianity's largest self-inflicted wound.

It was not inspired Jewish apostles or prophets at the Council of Nicea in 325 AD, who attached Bible names to this pagan doctrine from Babylon. This is where Constantine and Rome warped the identity of the Jewish God, and why the trinity doctrine is not found in the Bible. It was written by Romans over 200 years after the Bible! Numerous verses actually give this Catholic doctrine much difficulty. Let us explore this formerly Babylonian doctrine in the light of Scripture and in the historical aspect. The doctrine started in 325 AD, and they passed a law of death to anyone who thought or taught otherwise. They broke their own law about 60 years later when they rewrote it to include the Holy Spirit as a third and "equal" person! The version from 381 AD is the one we see today.

Some imply the word "trinity" is not found in Scripture, due to the fact the Hebrew language does not have a word for "trinity." First, isn't that a signal in itself? After several thousand years of Israel and the Lord being together, how can the Catholics and Protestants come along and re-define the identity of the Jewish God? How can we re-write God's identity "better than" the Jewish language and Scripture already have? And then accuse the Jews of not understanding their own God? The very Bible we quote and memorize was written by Jews!

Second, the Hebrew language does have the terminology to express the number "three," and the word "persons" if, and only if, it did describe their God. It doesn't.

Third, God is never referred to as "persons, members or three" in the Bible. Neither does the Bible ever refer to God as "they or them." The Bible does not say anywhere, nor even imply that God is three persons yet one God. A lie that is told often enough can become the truth. Scripture is very clear on God's identity. Let me ask, who is the Lord? (Deut. 6:4) (John 13:13)

Throughout history, why have Babylon (Nimrod, Semiramus, Tammuz); Egypt (Osiris, Isis, Horus); Greece (Zeus, Athena, Apollo); India (Brahama, Shiva, Vishnu); Rome (Jupiter, Venus, Mars); Catholics (Father, Son, Dove) and Protestants been the main promoters of a three person triad deity, but not Israel? That is because the Jewish Religion (Messianic believers included) has one God, period. Who do you think Messiah was? The Lord did not reproduce and have offspring. That isn't what Messiah means.

The Pharisees were mad and wanted to kill Messiah because He claimed to be (and was) YHVH, God of Israel (John 10:33). They also understood that Yeshua then claimed to be the One who gave the Torah to Moses and the Israelites, which is YHVH, their Creator; and they tried to seize Him again (verse 34).

We must remember, that according to the Jewish faith, (whose God we worship) the terms Messiah, Christ, Anointed, Son of God, Son of Man and Emmanuel (with us is YHVH) only meant one thing. It meant God had visited and redeemed His people, not that He split into three persons in order to do so. Did you notice how Zacharias (Luke 1:67, 68) refers to the baby (soon to be born) as the "Lord God of Israel"? He knew he would see the beginnings of Messiah's arrival before he died. It was Zacharias' son named John (Luke 1:76-80) who would prepare the way for God (YHVH) (Isa. 40:3).

Who does the prophet (Micah 5:2) say will be born in Bethlehem? The Ruler in Israel, to be born in Bethlehem, (Messiah) whose goings forth are from "old" (before time), from "age everlasting" (indefinite time). Yeshua the Messiah is none other than Yahveh God of Israel. Anyway, where is a verse that says Messiah was the "co-eternal Son of God"? It says He was the "begotten" on a certain day, (Heb. 1:5) but is never called an eternal Son, or "God the Son."

It was never a question in Scripture if Yeshua was the second member of the trinity. The decision to be made was, if He was Yahveh God performing the prophesied visit as Messiah. Even His name Yeshua, means YHVH Saviour or God saves. Does this shed some light on, (John 5:43) "I come in my Father's name"? What was the Father's name He came in? Yeshua. Did you know the word Yeshua was used over 100 times in the Old Testament? Look up the word "salvation" in your concordance. The Hebrew word "Yeshua" is translated "salvation" in English.

Isaiah and Hosea say YHVH is our only Saviour (Isa. 43:3, 11) (Isa. 45:21) (Hos. 13:4). Now compare the interchangeable meaning how (Titus 1:3, 4) and (Titus 2:10) refer to our Saviour. Yeshua is called "our great God and Saviour" (Titus 2:13).

What is the verse (Isa. 9:6) you read every Dec. 25th? "For unto us a child is born, a Son is given...His name shall be called Wonderful Counselor, the Mighty God, Everlasting Father, Prince of Peace." The Messiah is called the Mighty God and the Everlasting Father. When Phillip asked to see the Father,

Yeshua responded, "He that hath seen Me has seen the Father" (John 14:9). Have you ever prayed to God by calling Him...Father Jesus?

What about the word "Godhead" in the Bible? There are only three places this word is used. The very singular meanings can be found in your concordance. It means "that which is divine" in (Acts 17:29); "divinity" in (Rom. 1:20); "deity" in (Col. 2:9).

Does the Bible say we have to accept the trinity doctrine without question? (Acts 17:11) (Titus 1:9) Why do explanations of the trinity leave us even more confused? Explanations such as, "the three of them share equal power and equal glory, they never argue with each other, or they always agree with each other." A couple more blasphemous statements are, "We will see the three of them in heaven, or the three of them are of the same essence and relate to each other intimately." Where does the Bible use "each other" or the word "they" to describe God?

If someone's ecclesiastical explanation of the trinity gets to be such theological, hermeneutical, philosophical, barf-illogical gobbledygook that you cannot understand it, beware! We do not have to go to ten years of seminary to understand God's identity. A child should be able to get it. How did they explain the Gospel so that 3,000 people (Acts 2:41) understood enough about God to make a conversion decision in just one day?

Try thinking that every place you read "God," it has to mean three persons. You will find this does not make any sense, or fit the context, or fit the meaning of the Scriptures. And I don't recall ever reading a verse where Messiah instructed His disciples to kill anyone who would not accept He was the second member of a three person YHVH, do you?

You cannot identify a cult on the basis of non-acceptance of the trinity doctrine. This would start the Inquisition and Crusades all over again. Centuries ago, it was a death penalty to "not" believe in the trinity. Even the Protestant Movement continued the persecution of non-Trinitarians for years. Look up the Blasphemy Act, Act of Toleration and the Doctrine of the Trinity

Act. Yes, there is a difference between the Roman Catholic god and the Jewish God in the Bible. Why are people so willing to believe in a triune doctrine about YHVH that cannot be explained or understood, and is contradictory to the Bible?

Then we have the question, if Yeshua is God, "Who" was the Father that Messiah prayed to? Yeshua gives us the answer at the tomb of Lazarus (John 11:42). What Messiah said and taught about the Father was for the benefit of the people there; so they would believe Messiah was sent from God. Essentially, Messiah (the Son) is/was the Father extending Himself into the earth He created; as an "in the flesh" representation of Himself. What Yeshua said and did was our example, for our understanding and for our benefit; to relay what the Father wished to say and teach to mankind through His human visitation as Messiah.

Scripture never compares God to an egg (yolk-white-shell) or to water (ice-liquid-steam). These examples of the trinity are so lame. Anyway, the same water is not found in all three states simultaneously. And besides the yolk, white and shell, an egg has two membranes and an umbilicus; that's six parts! When we worship God, (Isa. 42:8) do the three of them divide our praise up equally? Does the "three of them" even sound biblical? When you pray to the Father, do the other two persons feel left out? When does anyone pray to the Holy Spirit (Ruach Hakodesh) as a person separate from the Lord?

Martin Luther had been a participant of Roman Catholic teaching for years before he decided to object publicly. After his learned protest against 95 points of Catholicism, he thought the Council of Nicea was correct about the trinity. Should we be embracing the trinity doctrine without question, from the very same institution that was so vehemently protested by Luther?

Let's not forget John Calvin and Michael Servetus. Servetus was killed at the stake in Switzerland on Oct. 27, 1553, for the crime of believing in One God and not in the trinity. Though Calvin believed in the trinity, he regularly denied the Hebrew Old Testament supported the trinity doctrine at all. Calvin was honest enough not to misinterpret "elohim" to try to justify his belief. John Calvin was the principal accuser and chief prosecutor in the trial, though the court did the sentencing. Servetus equated Calvin's belief in the trinity to that of Cerberus, the Greek mythological three headed dog guarding the gates of hell, and his conviction cost him his earthly life.

Sir Isaac Newton was an earnest Bible scholar. Even though this was well into the Protestant Movement, there were still penalties in his day if you did not believe in the trinity. Newton knew enough about Scripture to know the trinity doctrine was not biblical and his writings reflect it, but he kept quiet about it.

Some imply "elohim" denotes the trinity (Gen. 1:26). If this is true, why are Chemosh (Jud. 11:24), Dagon (Jud. 16:23), Baal-berith (Jud. 8:33), Baal-zebub (2 Ki. 1:2, 3), Nisroch (2 Ki. 19:37) and Ashtoreth (1 Ki. 11:5) all called elohim? God told Moses, I made you like "elohim" to Pharaoh (Exod. 7:1). Does that make Moses and these pagan gods also "three persons, yet one god," just because of the Hebrew word "elohim"?

And God said, "let us make man in our image" (Gen. 1:26). If God was talking, wouldn't whoever He was speaking to, or whoever was listening, certainly "not" be God? What does the very next verse say? And He made man in His own image (Gen. 1:27). Rather singular, don't you think? Is it the same with (Gen. 3:22, 11:7)? What about the Lord talking with the host of heaven (1 Kings 22:19-22) and they carrying on conversation with the Lord? It is obvious, whether the Lord is visiting Abraham or Joshua in a human body, or the Lord is being nailed to a cross in a human body; or the Lord is having conversation with His angels (not multiple persons of Himself); in whatever form He takes, He is still considered to be the Lord.

Why is God called "the Father," (Matt. 1:18, 20) when it was the Holy Spirit that did the conceiving in Mary? Doesn't this make the Holy Spirit the Father? But wait, Yeshua said "He" was the Father (John 14:9). Are all three of them the Father? Does "three fathers" even sound biblical? We all know that God is Spirit (John 4:24). The Ruach Hakodesh (Holy Spirit) is obviously Spirit. Does this mean there are two Spirit persons

126

within the God of Abraham? Do you have a verse for that? There are verses that mention the "Spirit of Yeshua" (Acts 16:7) (Rom. 8:9) (Phil. 1:19) (1 Pet. 1:11). Did you notice the terms "Spirit of God" and "Spirit of Christ" (Rom. 8:9) is used interchangeably in one sentence? Does this make three Spirit persons making up the God of Israel? I was under the impression there was just one Spirit (Eph. 4:4).

We all know that God (YHVH) was in Messiah, reconciling the world unto Himself (2 Cor. 5:19). God was also in the burning bush (Exod. 3:2-4), and in the pillar of a cloud (Exod. 13:21) and in the pillar of fire (Exod. 13:21). Do these other manifestations make Him six persons yet one God in hex-unity? There are folks who differentiate between YHVH visiting in a human form as a Theophony, or in human form another time as a Christophony. If God does not change, isn't this just creating a difference between former appearances of God and Messiah?

Some say that all three members of the trinity were present at Yeshua's baptism. Does this mean that two persons of the trinity (Yeshua and the Holy Spirit descending) were on the earth, while God the Father stayed in the heavens? But wait, we just read God was in Messiah, reconciling the world unto Himself (2 Cor. 5:19). Does this mean that all three trinity persons were in Yeshua while He was on the earth?

Is God so limited that, while as Messiah, He could not make a voice come out of heaven? Nothing was seen, only heard. At the same time, He caused a visible something to flutter down, imitating a dove's flight (John 1:32-34). Can God do this without having to be split into three persons in order to explain it? This was a vision for John to confirm he was baptizing (Is. 40:3) and preparing the way for YHVH, the one who sends His Spirit upon mankind. It does not say that any onlookers saw it also.

Historically, there is no evidence of the triad deity previous to Babylon (2000-1500 BC). It is also found in the Egyptian worship system (1500-1000 BC). But, the trinity was never a part of the Jewish or Messianic worship until Rome (325 AD) attached Bible names to pagan doctrines at the council of Nicea.

127

This is the point in time when Christianity was paganized, or Mithraism was Christianized, whichever is more accurate. After 1520, when the reformers left the Roman church, the trinity doctrine was carried along to the Protestant churches. A bunch of Romans re-writing biblical doctrines and the identity of the Jewish God three centuries after the fact, are definitely not my church forefathers. My church forefathers are written about in the Bible, not in some Roman archives. Why do we blindly think Constantine knew more about the Bible than we do today?

Some have said the Babylonians and Egyptians had the triad god deity because they "must have stolen" it from the Jews. The triad mystery deity had been in pagan cultures for centuries but, was never a part of Jewish Scriptures. The Jews are well known for keeping their One God monotheism pure. Does it seem likely that the pagans derived the triad deity concept for their god, from the Jews; who believe and teach a totally opposite view? And if belief in the trinity doctrine (written in 381 AD) were important for salvation; all the people recorded in the New Testament were not properly converted!

There can be no doubt in our minds that an ancient Babylonian or Egyptian would be very comfortable in today's average place of worship. They would see crosses, crosses with a circle on it somewhere, images of doves, statues (idols), worship of the mother and child, observance of the winter solstice, mourning 40 days, eggs and round cakes used at the spring solstice, fish on Friday, confessionals, celibacy of priests, vain repetitions in prayer to the mother of god, halos (nimbus) and even a triad deity. The names have changed since ancient times, but some of the former pagan practices, doctrines and teachings have evolved into what we see today.

Here are various other researcher's findings and conclusions.

The Encyclopedia of Religion, ed. Mircea Eliade, Macmillan Publishing, 1987, Vol. 15, p. 54) "Theologians today are in agreement that the Hebrew Bible does not contain a doctrine of the Trinity. Theologians agree that the New Testament also does not contain an explicit doctrine of the Trinity."

The New Encyclopedia Britannica, 1985, Vol. 11, p. 928: "Neither the word Trinity nor the explicit doctrine appears in the New Testament."

Oxford Companion to the Bible, 1993, p. 782: "Because the Trinity is such an important part of later Christian doctrine, it is striking that the term does not appear in the NT. Likewise the developed concept of three coequal partners in the Godhead found in later creedal formulations cannot be clearly detected within the confines of the canon."

Illustrated Bible Dictionary, Intervarsity Press, Tyndale House Publishers, 1980, part 3, p. 1: "The word Trinity is not found in the Bible. It did not find a place formally in the theology of the church until the fourth century."

New Catholic Encyclopedia, 1967, Vol. 14, p. 299: "The formulation 'One God in three Persons' was not solidly established, certainly not fully assimilated into Christian life and its profession of faith, prior to the end of the 4th century. Among the Apostolic Fathers, there had been nothing even remotely approaching such a mentality or perspective."

New Catholic Encyclopedia 1967, Vol. 14, p. 304: "The Trinity is not directly and immediately the Word of God."

New Catholic Encyclopedia, 1967, Vol. 14, p. 306: "The doctrine of the Trinity is not taught in the Old Testament."

The Catholic Encyclopedia, 1912, Vol. 15, p. 47: "In Scripture there is yet no single term by which the Three Divine Persons are denoted together."

The above Catholic statements are from the ones who wrote the trinity doctrine, and for centuries have killed to uphold and stand behind it. Then, their official assessment is that it cannot be found in the Bible, but they still require that you believe it or you will be shunned as a heretic! Sadly today, there are well meaning church folk still maintaining this mindset since the Protestant Movement. And I honestly don't recall reading a verse in the Bible about Messiah ever instructing the disciples to kill anyone who would not accept that He was the second member of a three person YHVH. This violent aggression toward those who do not agree with the trinity doctrine is a direct biblical contradiction to "loving your neighbor/enemy."

Encyclopedia of Religion and Ethics, ed. James Hastings, 1922, Vol. 6, p. 254: "There is in the Old Testament no indication of distinctions in the Godhead; it is an anachronism to find either the doctrine of the Incarnation or that of the Trinity in its pages."

Encyclopedia of Religion and Ethics, Vol. 12, p. 461: "At first the Christian faith was not Trinitarian. It was not so in the apostolic and sub-apostolic ages, as reflected in the New Testament and other early Christian writings."

The Encyclopedia of Religion, ed. Mircea Eliade, Macmillan Publishing, 1987, Vol. 15, p. 54: "Theologians today are in agreement that the Hebrew Bible does not contain a doctrine of the Trinity. Theologians agree that the New Testament also does not contain an explicit doctrine of the Trinity."

Edmund J. Fortman, The Triune God, Baker Book House, 1972: "The Old Testament tells us nothing explicitly or by necessary implication of a Triune God who is Father, Son and Holy Spirit. There is no evidence that any sacred writer even suspected the existence of a [Trinity] within the Godhead."

"To see in the Old Testament suggestions, foreshadowing's or 'veiled signs' of the Trinity of persons; is to go beyond the words and intent of the sacred writers. The Old Testament is strictly monotheistic. The idea that a Trinity is to be found there is utterly without foundation."

Edmund J. Fortman, The Triune God: "The New Testament writers give us no formal or formulated doctrine of the Trinity, no explicit teaching that in one God there are three equal divine persons. Nowhere do we find any Trinitarian doctrine of three distinct subjects of divine life and activity in the same Godhead."

130

The Encyclopedia Americana, p. 1956, p. 2941: "Fourth-century Trinitarianism did not reflect accurately early Christian teaching regarding the nature of God; it was on the contrary, a deviation from this teaching."

Bernard Lohse, A Short History of Christian Doctrine, Philadelphia Fortress Press, 1966, p. 38: "As far as the New Testament is concerned, one does not find in it an actual doctrine of the Trinity."

New International Encyclopedia, Vol. 22, page 476: "The trinity doctrine is not found in its fully developed form in the Scriptures. Modern theology does not seek to find it in the Old Testament."

Dictionary of the Bible by Scriptures, Vol. 1, p. 241: (on baptism) "The original form of words was, 'into the name of Jesus Christ or Lord Jesus.' Baptism into the trinity was a latter development."

The New International Dictionary of New Testament Theology, ed. Colin Brown, Zondervan, 1976, Vol. 2, p. 84: "The New Testament does not contain the developed doctrine of the Trinity."

Arthur Weigall, The Paganism in Our Christianity, 1928, p. 197: "The early Christians however, did not at first think of applying the Trinity idea to their own faith. There was no thought of three being an actual Trinity, coequal and united in One."

Arthur Weigall, The Paganism in our Christianity, G.P. Putnam and Sons, 1928, p. 198: "Jesus Christ never mentioned such a phenomenon, and nowhere in the New Testament does the word Trinity appear. The idea was only adopted by the Church three hundred years after the death of our Lord."

New International Dictionary of New Testament Theology, Vol. 2, p. 84: "Primitive Christianity did not have an explicit doctrine of the Trinity such as was subsequently elaborated in the creeds."

A.B. Davidson, Hastings Dictionary of the Bible, Vol. II, p. 205: "The Old Testament can scarcely be used as authority for the existence of distinctions within the Godhead."

William Smith, Dictionary of the Bible, ed. Peloubet, MacDonald Pub. Co., 1948, p. 220: "The fanciful idea that Elohim referred to the Trinity of persons in the Godhead hardly finds now a supporter among scholars. It is either what the grammarians call the plural of majesty, or it denotes the fullness of divine strength, the sum of the powers displayed by God."

The American Journal of Semitic Language and Literature, 1905, Vol. XXI, p. 208: "Elohim must rather be explained as an intensive plural, denoting greatness and majesty."

Emil Brunner, Christian Doctrine of God, Dogmatics, Vol. 1, p. 226: "No Apostle would have dreamed of thinking that there are three divine Persons."

Word Book Encyclopedia, Vol. 16, p. 7270: "The doctrine of the three in one is considered to be a mystery for which there is not adequate explanation."

Word Bible Commentary: "It is now universally admitted that the use of the plural in (Gen. 1:26) did not mean to the author that God was more than one Person."

There are still some Protestant denominations that sing the Doxology and Gloria Patri in their services. The Doxology was written in 1674 by a priest, Thomas Ken. The Gloria Patri is used for Eucharistic prayers, liturgy and Catholic devotions, like Novenas and the Rosary. These are blatantly Trinitarian statements that have found their way into Protestant services without serious examination. The Bible only said "Holy Spirit" (pneuma), meaning Ruach. The term "Holy Ghost" was added by the KJV translators and is not found in the original text.

Seraphim say, "holy, holy, holy" to YHVH (Isa. 6:1-3). Yeshua is the Almighty, who was, is, and is to come (Rev. 1:8); and the seraphim say to Him on the throne, holy, holy, holy (Rev. 4:8)

How did Messiah respond (Matt. 4:7) (Luke 4:12) to the devil's tempting? "It is written, you shall not tempt the Lord your God." Who was the devil tempting in this passage? Yeshua, the Lord your God!

The terms used for YHVH in the Old Testament are exactly the same terms used for Yeshua in the New Testament. Compare the terminology in these groups of verses.
The Lord (YHVH) is our Father (Isa. 63:16) (Isa. 64:8).
Yeshua the Lord is our Father (Isa. 9:6) (John 14:8, 9).

El Shaddai is the Almighty (Gen. 17:1).
Yeshua the Lord is the Almighty (Rev. 1:7, 8).

The God (YHVH) of Israel is the Shepherd (Ps. 23:1).
Yeshua the Lord is the good Shepherd (John 10:11, 14).

The Lord is the "I Am" (Exod. 3:14). (Not the... We Are!)
Yeshua the Lord is the "I Am" (John 8:58) (John: 18:5, 6).

YHVH said to keep His commandments (Exod. 20:4).
The Lord said to keep His commandments (John. 14:15, 21).

Every knee shall bow to the Lord (YHVH) of Israel (Isa. 45:23).
Every knee shall bow to Yeshua (Rom. 14:11) (Phil. 2:10, 11).

Jerusalem's King comes riding on a donkey (Zech. 9:9).
Yeshua the King rode a donkey (Matt. 21:5) (Luke 19:35).

The Lord God (YHVH) of Israel sits on His throne (Ps. 45:6).
Yeshua the Lord sits on the throne (Heb. 1:8) (Rev. 7:17).

The God of Israel will come with all His Holy ones (Zech. 14:5).
Yeshua the Lord is coming with all His saints (1 Thess. 3:13).

The Lord God of Israel's Words will endure forever (Isa. 40:8).
Yeshua's words will endure forever (Matt. 24:35) (Mark 13:31).

The Lord God (YHVH) of Israel does not change (Mal. 3:6).
Yeshua the Lord does not change (Heb. 13:8).

The Lord God of Israel is our Comforter (Isa. 51:12) (Isa. 66:13).
Yeshua the Lord is our Comforter (John 14:18).

The God of Israel raised Yeshua from the dead (Romans 10:9).
Yeshua the Lord raised Himself from the dead (John 2:19-21).

The YHVH of Israel is our Saviour (Isa. 43:3, 11) (Isa. 45:15, 21)
(Hos. 13:4).
Yeshua the Lord is our only Saviour (Eph. 3:23) (Titus 1:4)
(Titus 2:13).

Only the Lord God (YHVH) of Israel forgives our sins (Ps. 85:2).
Yeshua the Lord forgives our sins (Mark 2:5-7).

The Lord God (YHVH) of Israel is the first and the last (Isa. 44:6).
Yeshua the Lord is the first and the last (Rev. 1:8, 17, 18).

We have faith in the Lord God (YHVH) of Israel (1 Pet. 1:21).
We have faith in Yeshua the Lord (Gal. 2:16, 3:26) (Col. 2:12).

The Lord God of Israel is the Creator (Gen. 1:1) (Mal. 2:10).
The Spirit (Ruach) of God is the Creator (Job 33:4).
Yeshua the Lord is the Creator (John 1:10) (Heb. 1:2).

The Lord God (YHVH) of Israel alone controls the wind and the
waves (Ps. 89:9) (Isa. 51:15).
Messiah the Lord controlled the wind and waves in front of His
disciples (Luke 8:25).

The Lord God of Israel is our Redeemer (Ps. 78:35) (Isa. 47:4).
Yeshua the Lord is our Redeemer (Luke 1:68) (Titus 2:14).

The Lord of Israel is the King of Glory (Ps. 24:10) (Isa. 42:8).
Yeshua the Lord is the King of Glory (I Cor. 2:8).

The Lord God (YHVH) of Israel pours out His Spirit (Joel 2:28).
The Messiah (Lord) baptizes with the Holy Spirit (John 1:33).

The Lord God (YHVH) of Israel is the Lord our God (Deut. 6:4).
Yeshua is the Lord our God (John 13:13 and 20:28).

The Lord (YHVH) is our Rock (2 Sam. 22:2, 3, 47) (Ps. 18:31).
Yeshua the Lord is our Rock (Matt. 16:18) (1 Cor. 10:4).

The Lord God (YHVH) of Israel is the Holy One (Isa. 43:14, 15).
Yeshua the Lord is the Holy One (Acts 3:14).

YHVH is the One Husband (Isa. 54:5) (Jer. 31:32).
Yeshua the Lord is the One Husband (2 Cor. 11:2).

YHVH is the Lord of lords (Deut. 10:17).
Yeshua the Messiah is the Lord of lords (Rev. 19:16).

We only "serve" YHVH (Deut. 10:20).
Yeshua said only God can be "served" (Matt. 4:10) (Luke 4:8).
We only "serve" Yeshua the Lord (Acts 27:23) (Rom. 14:18)
(Col. 3:24).

We cannot worship any other god except YHVH, the Lord God
of Israel (Exod. 34:14).
Yeshua declared only YHVH can be worshiped (Matt. 4:10)
(Luke 4:8).
Many people worshiped Yeshua without any rebuke (Matt. 2:11;
8:2; 9:18; 14:33; 15:25; 20:20; 28:9; 28:17) (John 9:38).

Look at the prophecy about John the Baptist announcing the
arrival of Messiah (Isa. 40:3). Pay particular attention to the
terminology used for "Whom" John was announcing. All three
of these verses refer to Yeshua the Messiah as being the Lord
God of Israel (John 1:23) (Luke 3:4). How can we call Yeshua
our Lord, and call "Father God" from the Old Testament our
Lord too? Do we have two Lords? This cannot be.

Think about doubting Thomas' response, "my Lord and my
God" (my Kurios and my Theos) (John 20:28, 29). These are
terms that could only be said about YHVH, the Lord God of
Israel. Saying it about anyone else would be blasphemy.
Messiah blessed Thomas for seeing and believing. The obvious
point is we can only call our One God, the "Lord."

What if reward or penalty on Judgment Day hinges upon if you
135

worshiped God's (child) Son, the second member of the trinity named Jesus Christ from Rome? Or, did you worship Yeshua the Messiah, which is the Lord God of Israel manifest in human flesh? If this distinction were to be criteria for Judgment Day, it would be a bad day for many! How long waiver ye between these two opinions? (See 1 Kings 18:21)

How many verses does it take to disprove the false doctrine of "splitting God into three persons" in your mind? We are not grasping at straws here. If we can put a man on the moon and cheese in a can, why can't we understand Messiah of the Bible without adding the trinity doctrine to explain it? There can only be One Mighty Lord, who is our Everlasting Father, Who came as Messiah; and Who sends us His Spirit (Ruach) (Isa. 9:6). This is not difficult to understand.

I heard an intriguing statement from Islam ridiculing the trinity doctrine of Rome, and God having "a son" (the second member of the trinity). Islam was not ridiculing Israel because Israel does not have a trinity and on this point, they seem to know more about the identity of the Jewish God than the Christian world. Their statement: "God is so great; He would not have to reproduce and have offspring in order to accomplish His will."

Wasn't it just back around 1916, the Assembly of God denomination had a split? Folks did research and found the trinity doctrine came from Babylon. These people had been strict Trinitarians who realized an error and became non-Trinitarians, not the other way around. The people finding the trinity doctrine to be unscriptural became the United Pentecostal Church in 1945.

If the God of Israel were three persons, then everywhere in the Bible you read the word "God," it would have to mean the three persons forming one "deity." Open your Bible to any page, anywhere you see the word "God," try to apply three persons to it. You will find the trinity does not fit the Scriptures, or the context, or the meanings of the verses. The terminology used in almost every book in the New Testament disproves this man written doctrine, making it a contradiction to God's Word.

Think for a minute what their explanation actually entails. We believe in one God. God is the Father. Jesus is God. Jesus is not the Father. What kind of psycho-babble is that? Now insert "Lord" for the word "God" in the previous four statements. If Yahweh went to a costume party wearing a human Messiah disguise; would He have a different identity, or have split into three persons, or stopped being the omnipresent God? The trinity doctrine is nothing more than a deadly Catholic poison disguised as a counterfeit cure.

About 200 years ago the Mormons took the Jewish Bible, made a few changes and called it their own new religion. Years later, the Jehovah's Witnesses took the Jewish Bible, made some changes and called it their own new religion. Hasn't Rome and the Catholics done the same thing with the trinity doctrine since 325 AD, just for a longer period of time? The $64,000 question is; what was the definition and understanding of God's identity from 4000 BC to 100 AD; which includes Messiah, but was well before Roman Catholic influence and domination?

No, you do not have to understand this mysterious, inexplicable Roman written doctrine, because it is not in the Bible! Don't you think after thousands of years of being very clear about His identity, the Lord might have mentioned at least once, that He was three separate individual coequal co-eternal persons?

Baptism in the Name of the Father, Son and Holy Spirit

Here's what I thought I knew: We must follow the Great Commission given by the Lord Himself as the only prescribed method of baptism (Matt. 28:19). Any other words would not be what the Lord was indicating to the disciples.

Here's more to consider: We are not even going to discuss the evolution from dunking to sprinkling in Roman history. Baptism was and still is full immersion under the water. The book of Acts has four accounts of baptisms being carried out by the disciples and Paul (Acts 2:38, 8:16, 10:48, 19:5). You will notice they only baptized in the name of Yeshua. Not once did they use the words, "Father, Son and Holy Spirit." Why is this? Were they doing it wrong? Or, were they doing exactly what Yeshua commanded in the Great Commission? I have heard it said that it is better to follow the words the Lord quoted, rather than the words the disciples (who made mistakes) used. They told me if the disciples used words different from what the Lord indicated, then they were wrong. Folks, we got a big problem here! If the disciples and Paul were wrong, this puts the whole New Testament in question, because they wrote it!

We should also consider Sharp's Rule when reading translations from Greek to English. This will also greatly assist in understanding the lengthy salutations at the beginning and end of most of the letters in the New Testament. This will also help us understand many other statements and phrases throughout the text. You can easily verify Granville Sharp's Rule from 1798. Basically, when two or more nouns are linked by "and," if the Greek definite article before the first noun is not repeated in front of the second noun, it always refers back to the same identity (person, place or thing) stated by the first noun.

"Dictionary of the Bible by Scriptures" Vol. 1, page 241: "The original form of words was, into the name of Jesus Christ or Lord Jesus. Baptism into the trinity was a latter development."

For example, to baptize in the "name" of the Father, and of the (Messiah) Son, and of the (Ruach) Holy Spirit would be referring back to the singular name. This is verified by the words used by the disciples and Paul. They understood what the Lord had meant by this commission and now we can also know what it indicates and fulfills...Messiah was the Lord (YHVH) in human form, and not one of three separate individual persons.

Here is another example of Sharp's Rule: "the appearing of our great God and Saviour Jesus Christ" (Titus 2:13). The one conclusion that can be drawn from this verse is that Yeshua is our great God and Saviour. The disciples never baptized using the Trinitarian formula because it was written over 200 years after they lived!

I even heard someone say that on the day of Pentecost, when Peter said to repent and be baptized in the name of Yeshua (Acts 2:38), he was "mistaken" by not following the Lord's words in the Great Commission. If you look at (Acts 2:14), Peter stood up with the eleven (disciples). Matthew (who wrote Matthew 28:19) was right there when Peter said what he said. There is no record of any of the disciples rebuking Peter for saying it wrong, keeping in mind; they were all there together when the Lord gave them the Great Commission.

God Appearing in Human Form

Here's what I thought I knew: God the Father appearing, in human form in the Old Testament, is called a Theophony. This is different from God the Son appearing in human form in the New Testament, which is called a Christophony.

Here's more to consider: YHVH (God) is called the Lord when appearing in the Tanakh (Old Testament). And God is called the Lord when appearing in the New Testament as Messiah. The Lord may have appeared to numerous people in human form at least 30 different times before He came as Messiah.

Here is a list of all the instances I have found, to date. I may not have found them all; you may find or know of even more.
Gen. 3:8 - Adam & Eve – cool of the day
Gen. 12:7 – Abraham
Gen. 16:7-13 - Hagar
Gen. 17:1 – Abraham
Gen. 18: all – Abraham and Sarah
Gen. 26:2 – Isaac
Gen. 26:24 – Isaac
Gen. 32:24-30 – Jacob's name changed to Israel
Gen. 35:9 – Jacob
Exod. 3:2, 16 – Moses burning bush (Acts 7:30)
Exod. 33:23 – Moses
Exod. 34:5&6—Moses
Num. 22:9 – Balaam

Num. 22:20 – Balaam
Num. 22:22-35 – Balaam
Deut. 31:15 – Moses
Josh. 5:13-15 – Joshua
Judges 2:1-5 – Joshua and Israelites
Judges 6:22, 23 – Gideon
Judges 13:3 – Samson's Mom
Judges 13:9-20 – Samson's parents
1 Sam. 3:21 – Samuel
1 Sam. 3:10 – Samuel
2 Sam. 24:16, 17 – David – 2 Chron. 3:1
1 Kings 3:5 – Solomon
1 Kings 9:2 – Solomon
2 Kings 19:33-35 – slew 185,000
2 Chron. 1:7 – Solomon
2 Chron. 7:12 – Solomon
Jer. 31:3 – Jeremiah
Daniel 3: 25 – furnace

You will notice from the Hebrew terminology, there are a number of times where the human manifestation of God is referred to as the "Angel of the Lord."

It also says that the Lord was in the pillar of a cloud and in the pillar of fire as he led the Israelites through the wilderness. I am not sure if this qualifies as a human visitation. It also tells of the "Shekinah Glory" of the Lord appearing numerous times. The Lord spoke to them from the Glory. I do not think this qualifies as a human visitation either, but He sure did it a number of times in the wilderness.

Did you notice at first glance, (Josh. 5:13) Joshua couldn't even tell if He was friend or foe? Yet, He was still YHVH. Kind of like when He came as Messiah, huh? The question to ponder is: If a photograph were taken at each of these different events, wouldn't each of the 30 photographs of God look the same? Wouldn't He look the same to each of the different eye witnesses of His presence? And since the Lord changes not (Mal. 3:6), would these 30 photographs of YHVH look like Messiah did while He walked the earth? When we all see

140

Yeshua sitting on His throne, will the Old Testament believers say; yes, that's Him, but when He appeared to us, He didn't have the nail marks in His hands and feet?

If the 30 photographs reflected different faces, wouldn't these famed people of the Old Testament argue with the disciples about who the Lord actually is, had He looked differently? Wouldn't He look the same to all who had seen Him previously, (Rev. 7:17) especially when they see Him sitting on His throne?

It is obvious that whether the Lord is visiting Abraham in a human body, or sitting on His throne having conversation with His angels (1 Kings 22:19-22) or being nailed to a cross, He is still YHVH (Ps. 144:15).

The Kingdom of God – Now or Future?

Here's what I thought I knew: The Kingdom of God will not be in effect until the second coming of Messiah. Because the Jews weren't ready for the Kingdom and they rejected Messiah, He had to get nailed to a cross and the Kingdom was delayed until a future time.

Here's more to consider: Yeshua the Messiah came to usher in His Kingdom with the first coming. To think that rejection by "some of the Jews" (not all) would keep the Lord from accomplishing His intended plan is ludicrous. If the Lord knows the end from the beginning, didn't He know there was going to be rejection by some of the people? The Lord's rejection is predicted in prophecy (Ps. 22:16-18) (Ps. 118:22) (Isa. 53:3). Wouldn't predicting it 1,000 years in advance kind of prove it was His idea all along?

John the Baptist proclaimed, "Repent, for the Kingdom of heaven is at hand" (Matt. 3:2). After John's arrest, Yeshua preached, "The time is fulfilled and the Kingdom of God is at hand" (Mark 1:14, 15). The parallel account in Matthew says, "Repent, for the Kingdom of heaven is at hand" (Matt. 4:17).

Did Messiah think the Kingdom was at hand, but because of rejection by the Jews, He was mistaken? Did Messiah "say" the Kingdom was at hand, but know it would be delayed and it really wasn't at hand? Surely you jest! If Messiah failed to bring in the Kingdom with His first coming, how do we know He can do it on His second try? This is a distorted view. The Jews were sometimes blinded in part to understanding the writings of the prophets (Acts 13:27). Didn't the Scriptures testify of Messiah coming? Some recognized Him, yet some did not.

Obviously, the Jews expected a physical kingdom, with them superior over the nations. The rejection by some did not make Messiah "suffer" on the cross, as if crucifixion could have been avoided had He not been rejected. The cross was not a last minute surprise for the Lord. He could have summoned legions of angels, (Matt. 26:56) but then how would Scripture have been fulfilled? The cross and rejection by some was obviously in His plan all along (Luke 17:25) (Acts 17:3) (Acts 26:22, 23).

Had Messiah offered the kind of kingdom the Jews desired, as of Solomon or David, they probably would not have rejected Him. Even the Pharisees expected a physical kingdom when they questioned Messiah (Luke 17:20). He assured them the Kingdom was in their midst (Luke 17:21). See (Luke 11:20).

After Yeshua fed more than 5,000 people, He perceived they were going to try to force Him to be an earthly king and He withdrew to the hills alone (John 6:14, 15). The Lord did not usher in an earthly kingdom, but a "spiritual" Kingdom.

Yeshua said specifically there were those standing right there who would not die until they saw the Kingdom of God come with power (Mark 9:1). If Peter did not use the keys to the Kingdom on the day of Pentecost, then the people who were standing there waiting for the Kingdom should be getting really old by now! Then, in (Acts Chapter 10), Peter again uses the keys to open the Kingdom to the Gentiles.

No one can deny the future reality of His Kingdom, or that His Kingdom is everlasting. But, this does not nullify the fact that the Kingdom remains a current reality as well. Paul was aware the Kingdom was a present reality in his time (Rom. 14:17). Paul wrote to the Colossians, "We were delivered from the power of darkness and transferred to the Kingdom" (Col. 1:13, 14). From morning until night, Paul explained to them the Kingdom of God (Acts 28:23). While suffering tribulation, the apostle John was sure the Kingdom was a present reality (Rev. 1:9). Apparently Paul and John never heard the Kingdom had been postponed.

Unknown Tongues

Here's what I thought I knew: The only proof a person has been filled with the Holy Spirit is the evidence of them speaking in "unknown" tongues. This is sometimes called "the language of angels or a private prayer language," because it sounds like just guttural sounds, babble or gibberish.

Here's more to consider: The shocking fact is, in all six verses from the King James Bible that say "unknown tongues," the word "unknown" is in italics. That means the King James translators added it (1 Cor. 14:2, 4, 13, 14, 19, 27).

They were trying to convey the thought of languages "that have not been learned" by the speaker, and not some un-interpretable babble. Most Bibles since the KJV have discovered this addition and omitted the word "unknown." There are only three examples in the Bible when people actually spoke in other tongues (Greek-glossa-languages).

The first occasion was on the day of Pentecost when the disciples spoke and everyone heard them in their own "language" (Acts 2:7-11).

The second occasion was when the men at Cornelius' house received the Holy Spirit, spoke in other languages and magnified God (Acts 10:46).

The third occasion was when Paul laid his hands on them and

they spoke in other languages and prophesied (Acts 19:6). Did you notice each of these situations involved languages that were understood by the listeners? They heard them in their own languages, they magnified God and they prophesied. Prophesy is inspired speaking from God. It was done decently and in order.

Did Paul speak in the language of angels? That is not what the verse says (1 Cor. 13:1-3). Paul said "though," or (if) I speak in the languages of men and angels. The use of "though" in this context is a supposition. He also said, if I have the gift of prophecy, if I understand all mysteries and all knowledge, if I have all faith to move mountains, if I give my body to be burned and I don't have "love," I gain nothing. Paul's whole statement is hypothetical. He did not give his body to be burned, he was beheaded in Rome. I don't recall Paul claiming to understand all mysteries, having all knowledge or to have moved a mountain either. Surely moving a mountain would have been recorded in history. Anyway, whenever angels spoke to people, it wasn't angelic babble and the people understood what they said.

If you speak in a language that is not understood by the listeners, it does nobody any good (1 Cor. 14:9). If there is no person present to interpret, you are to keep silence in the church (1 Cor. 14:28). You are to talk silently with God, because this edifies no one but the speaker (1 Cor. 14:4). It is to be done in order, one at a time, to edify believers and non-believers alike "if" there is an interpretation. It was still a real language spoken, even if there was no interpretation or translation and the person was to remain silent.

If random bursting forth with unknown sounds and noises means something Spirit filled, then all my children spoke in tongues between 4 months and 1 year of age! There just wasn't an interpretation, so they should have kept silent.

Paul would rather speak five words that could be understood; than ten thousand (1 Cor. 14:19) in a "language" that could not be understood. One should desire rather to prophesy for edification of the surrounding believers and non-believers. The Delphi Oracles (drugged priestesses) of the pagan world would give epileptic like "ecstatic utterances" as a sign or message from the gods. Paul didn't want Christians to imitate this, because Oracles felt spiritual and praised of men with this self-glorying evidence of contact with God (1 Cor. 12:2).

Would this have had anything to do with a private heavenly prayer language of gibberish and babble? If it even remotely meant babble, it says not to do it out loud in the assembly. How can anyone possibly interpret babble? The person babbling may know what they are feeling or thinking while they are babbling; so why can't they share it in a language the people listening can understand and therefore be exhorted? It is supposed to bring glory to the Lord and not cause confusion to believers and potential believers alike.

There are many different languages, but they all have meaning (1 Cor. 14:10, 11). Paul wished they all spoke in tongues, which would imply some believers did not (1 Cor. 14:5). We should desire higher Spiritual gifts (1 Cor. 12:31). God gives gifts of different kinds (1 Cor. 12:27-31) to different people. Do all work miracles? Do all heal? Do all teach? Do all speak in languages? Do all interpret? The list of the fruits of being Spirit filled does not include speaking in tongues (Gal. 5:22-25).

I recall hearing a TV VIP rip off the same phrase in tongues so often I can almost recite it, "Honda de la shabba de la booshay." Was there an interpretation? Did anyone get edified (1 Cor. 14:6) beside the babbler? Did non-believers get drawn to the Saviour by hearing this message? By doing this, the person lets you know they "have" the gift of speaking in tongues. But, when you see this same person preaching in a foreign country, why do they need a translator on stage with them, if they have the gift of speaking in other languages?

I heard of a current day example of speaking in tongues that seems more in line with the biblical description. An African visitor who spoke very little English was visiting a family in the U.S. and attended a church service with them. In the middle of the sermon to her embarrassment, a lady blurted out an unusual stream of words. The knowledgeable pastor stopped and asked if anyone had an interpretation, to which no response. They dismissed it as they should. On the way home, the African visitor commented how nice it was that someone would welcome him to the church in his own native language. The visitor was edified with a real language, and at the next meeting the whole congregation was edified when they received the interpretation and the story. The lady, who spoke a real language she did not learn, was not embarrassed any longer (edified) for being used for the Lord's purpose. This example seems more biblical than sister such-n-much or brother got-it-goin'-on spouting out a few indistinguishable words in a sermon or from a pew; and moving on without any attempt to interpret, translate or expound.

Altar Calls

Here's what I thought I knew: Anyone who wants to give their life to the Lord or re-dedicate their life to the Lord, please come forward. You have to take the first steps down the aisle to come to the Lord.

Here's more to consider: Nobody is saved as the result of an altar call. Going forward and answering a couple questions correctly, or reciting a few choice sentences does not save a person. Though there is nothing wrong with going forward, salvation comes by faith in Messiah and what is already done, and not from following a prescribed ritual.

If a person does not go down the aisle to an altar call, does this mean they cannot have a life changing experience with the Lord? Are you kidding? The altar call is a recent phenomenon, less than 200 years in practice. If altar calls were necessary for salvation; that would mean all the people from Yeshua to the early 1800's were not properly converted.

Charles Finney seems to be the originator of this manner of

score-boarding how many souls were saved at the last service. This altar call was eventually used to collect success data on how effective their tent meetings, camp meetings and revival meetings were. They wanted to know how many souls were saved. Most did not follow up on these conversions to see if the ones who came forward actually lived changed lives thereafter. It was a way to keep track of what good things these men felt they were doing for God, and probably not an outward show of ego.

They even saved the seats up front, calling them the mourner's bench or anxious seat, for those who were repentant. Charles Spurgeon was adamantly against the altar call. Other notable evangelists such as Jonathan Edwards, George Whitefield and John Wesley, who lived before this exercise was invented, never even heard of altar calls.

A few of the folks who used this altar call technique in the past, and helped it grow into what we see today were: Peter Cartwright, Bob Jones, R.A. Torrey, Sam Jones, John R. Rice, Billy Sunday and Billy Graham. Now we see many pastors adopting this activity. What about the folks who go down the aisle numerous times, but their lives show no change? What about the folks who stay in their pew, but go home and live a new life changed by our Saviour?

There is a manipulative aspect incorporated into this man made exercise. Many preachers are actually taught to save some heart wrenching or tear jerking story until the sermon is nearly over. After building up the congregation's emotions, the lights may dim, the organist plays softly and the call is made for all who have a need to come forward. This is intentionally and almost deceptively evoking a response.

The verse sometimes used to support the altar call is, "if you confess Me before men, I will confess you before the Father" (Matthew 10:32). This verse has nothing to do with the conversion experience of confessing the Lord for the first time. This describes how disciples should witness for the Lord "after" the conversion experience. Why would the public display of walking down the aisle be the important factor in someone's salvation? If anything, wouldn't baptism and a life changed be the more obvious and biblical outward show of an inner commitment? So, whether someone accepts the Lord at an altar call or does not walk down an aisle at all; their belief in and acceptance of what was done on the cross and by Whom, is what saves. A life changed by His grace is the following result.

Slain in the Spirit

Here's what I thought I knew: Falling or "being pushed" on the forehead backwards, writhing, shaking and twitching on the ground, making weird noises or laughing incessantly is called being filled with the Spirit or being drunk in the Spirit. They sometimes use "I fell at his feet as if dead" as support for this behavior (Rev. 1:17).

Here's more to consider: Let's look at the verse people misuse to promote this questionable phenomenon (Rev. 1:17). John was at the Lord's feet, in complete understanding and listening to what the Lord had to say. The Lord was there to reveal something to John, not to push him backward while focusing on "that" experience.

The biblical examples are always falling on your face before God. When paying homage or respect to someone, one always bows forward or falls on their face, forward. Falling back and worse events are actions that demon possessed people exhibited before they were exorcised. When delivered, they sat quietly in their right mind (Mark 5:15) (Luke 8:35, 36).

I remember in the early 1980's, J. Vernon McGee warned of this extremism starting to creep into the church. This display was sometimes coined "the Toronto blessing." It didn't take long for this trend to grow into what is now called "drunk in the spirit." They may have been drunk, but in what spirit? There was some big TV church in Florida that promoted this before being exposed for electronic trickery. Then I started seeing others lending credence to this elsewhere. One must ask how a non-believer would be drawn to our Lord by witnessing this nonsense. I have spoken with believers and non-believers alike who were repelled and repulsed by this outward carnal display of fleshly exhibitionism.

How can someone wind up like a pro baseball pitcher and throw the Holy Spirit across the stage like a fast ball? Then a suspiciously obliging person leaps off his feet onto his back, just a-shaking and a-twitching. How can this act of flopping around like a fish out of water be construed as Spirit filled glory? I wish Paul and the disciples were here to give their opinion on things we see today (1 Cor. 14:26, 33, 40).

They will even use the verse about the laying on of hands to try and support this outrageous behavior (Acts 8:17). Every time people were filled with the Spirit in the Bible, they magnified God while remaining in complete control. They acted happy and joyous, and not flopping around like epileptic crazed loons. It was done decently and in order and not in some orchestrated, exaggerated freak show fashion.

Have you noticed pure hearted children who wait expectantly to share in and be a part of this experience? They watch adults convulse, shake and fall down; but when the preacher touches the child, nothing happens. Does the child feel left out or unworthy because it didn't happen to them? Could this activity confuse or disappoint children and other potential believers away from the Lord?

Secret Bible Codes

Here's what I thought I knew: The assassinations of Abraham Lincoln, John F. Kennedy and Yitzhak Rabin are predicted by secret Bible codes. Supposedly there are many other hidden messages encoded in the text that we should consider just as valid as Scripture. We believers "should be" paying specific attention to their enlightening meanings.

149

Here's more to consider: It seems very suspicious these codes are only available to the generation that has a computer at their disposal and was unknown to all believers previous to now. If we had known of these predictions earlier, could we have prevented the assassinations? Could we have protected these famous men from their respective deaths?

Michael Drosnin wrote the "The Bible Code," which uses numerical sequences of letters from Bible books to make words and messages from them. An article in "USA Today" (4 June, 1997) stated his claims are unreliable. Obviously, he did not include words such as "picnic, happy, zebra, catalog, aardvark, barbeque, dishwasher, fantasy, foolish, bizarre and imaginary" as important coded messages from God. These words can be found in code just as easily as the other names.

Let's examine the method in which these supposed "Bible secrets" were derived. By counting every third, fourth or whatever letter through a book or books of the Bible, one can come up with a great number of words. How can we know which words are important Godly messages? What about coming up with one word by counting every third letter, and then the next word is from counting every twenty-sixth letter? Sometimes they will count every 50th letter or more to come up with a supposed word to fit their hidden message. How can the two words be associated together by using different numerical searching sequences?

Or, sometimes they go front to back for one word, and then bottom to top for the next word. Then they think they really came up with some great secret. Then the very next word was obtained diagonally. Is there inconsistency here?

There is another big problem with this method. The Bible code searchers will use one word from the Hebrew language, and then bring up the next word found in the English language to complete the coded information. This is insane! There are about 850,000 words in the Bible. Could you come up with a good "Word Search" puzzle with so many letters at your disposal? Should we use Hebrew, Greek, English or some other language to uncover these hidden meanings? How about a combination of several languages? Oh, I guess they already are!

Another point to ponder; the Hebrew language does not incorporate the vowels, so how do these coded messages have vowels in them? By using this broad spectrum, I could extract special messages out of a Sports Illustrated magazine or the daily newspaper. In fact, using the Bible code method, some Professor took a copy of the novel "Moby Dick" and found the predictions of 13 assassinations of different presidents, prime ministers and other important figures!

Are the Bible codes really so spectacular if the messages are only discovered after the fact? These code searchers spend so much time looking for secret messages, they could be missing meanings right there in front of them; what the Bible is really talking about and what it actually means.

Da Vinci's Painting. The Last Supper

The next time you see Da Vinci's painting of the last supper; take a closer look. The shape and design of the table and chairs are Medieval and not a correct depiction of the reclining tables for the time and culture of Messiah. It is no stretch of the imagination to detect all the people appear to be Caucasian. An observant eye will also notice that there are no prayer shawls (tallit) visible, or much of anything else that is Jewish in appearance.

According to the Bible, there could have been fifteen or more people present; (Mark 14:19, 20) but the painting only shows thirteen. Technically, it was not His "last" supper, it was the Passover meal. The gospels relay the Lord ate meals (suppers) "after" His resurrection.

Let's look at the most glaring discrepancies displayed in this famous painting. Check out the brightly lit outdoor scenery

151

pictured in the windows behind them. If it was the Passover meal, it would have been after sundown and dark outside.

Now look at the food on the dishes. There should be roast lamb for the meal, but Da Vinci's artwork displays fish on the plates! If it was the Passover meal, the bread would have been unleavened, like a big flat saltine cracker. But the artist pictured puffy bread rolls made with yeast (leaven).

The painting appears to have a nimbus (halo) around the Lord's head, which originates from a pagan symbol of sun-god worship. Da Vinci used these to identify holy people in many of his paintings.

It is probably true that Da Vinci used townspeople to pose for the different faces in the painting, which would be why they appear to be European and do not look Jewish. But it is probably only a rumor that the person who posed for Jesus' face, was the same one who also posed for Judas' face.

CHAPTER SEVEN

Bible Questions and Answers

Here is a collection of assorted facts and other interesting information I happened upon along the way. I'm going to put them in a question and answer format to make it more interesting for study. Here they are in no particular order.

What King ate grass, grew hair like eagle feathers and nails like a bird talons for seven years? King Nebuchadnezzar (Dan. 4:31-33).

Did Delilah cut Samson's hair? No, Delilah did not cut his hair. She called a man to shave the braids (Judges 16:19).

What name appears most often in the Bible? The answer is David, which shows up around 1135 times. The name Jesus shows up around 977 times.

What verse is known as the Shema (Sh'ma)? The Shema is one of the major verses in the Jewish religion (Deut. 6:4). Hear O' Israel, the Lord our God, the Lord is one. Here it is in Hebrew: Shema Israel Adonai Eloheinu Adonai Echad.

How long was Yeshua on the cross? From when to when? He was on the cross from 9am to 3pm (Mark 15:25, 33, 34).

What word is pronounced the same and means the same thing in every land on earth? Hallelujah means the same thing worldwide and is regarded as the highest word of praise.

What name "should" be pronounced the same and mean the same thing in every land on earth? Yeshua; which is the name of the Lord.

What is the root of all evil? Money is not the root of all evil. It is the <u>love</u> of money that is the root of all evil (1 Tim. 6:10).

Did Saul seek out a witch at Endor? It was not a witch. It was a woman that had a familiar spirit, or a medium (1 Sam. 28:7).

How many times was the term Holy Ghost used when the New Testament was written? None. When written, it was always the word Ruach or Spirit (in the Greek, pneuma). The King James translators seemed to haphazardly insert the word Ghost for Spirit, at their whim and whimsy. Where in Scripture is God ever called a ghost?

What prophet did Yeshua quote most often? Isaiah.

What did Peter do when the Lord told him to "lower his nets"? When the Lord said "nets," Peter let down his "net" (Luke 5:5 KJV). Of course, when Peter did not follow the Lord's instruction, the net (singular) broke. When he needed his partners to help, both boats began to sink (Luke 5:7, 8).

What unusual cargo did Moses take out of Egypt? Per request, Moses took Joseph's bones (Exod. 13:19).

Why was the "calf" the form chosen for an idol by Aaron and the Israelites? Can you name it? The Israelites had just spent hundreds of years in slavery in Egypt. They had incorporated some of the Egyptian gods and idols they had seen for many years into their worship. The Egyptians had a bull/calf god named Apis.

What did Moses do with the golden calf? Moses melted the calf in the fire, ground the gold into powder, threw the powder in the water and made the people drink the water (Exod. 32:20).

Was Moses aware of God's "Book of Life"? God said He would blot out those who sinned against Him (Exod. 32:32, 33).

Approximately how many verses in the Bible are about Baal and the Babylon worship system? There are approximately 1,000 verses about Baal and the Babylon system. With so many verses, do you think God wants us to be aware of what it has influenced, how it has evolved and what it has become today?

154

Which disciple was known as "old camel knees"? Whether from his normal physical appearance, or from kneeling so much in prayer; James was known as old camel knees.

How long did it take for the plant to grow that shaded Jonah? The plant sprang up overnight and a worm made it die the very next night (Jonah 4:6, 10).

Did the axe head really float for Elisha? The man showed Elisha where the axe head had fallen into the water. If the miracle were for the iron to float, there was no need for the prophet to cut down a stick. The miracle was that the prophet threw the stick, which landed in the hole of the axe the first try and made it surface (2 Kings 6:5, 6). The man worried to lose a borrowed axe because iron may have been rare at the time.

Who told the woman to get all the neighbors jars so they could be filled with oil? The prophet Elisha made sure the widow had enough oil to sell and pay her debts, keep her sons out of slavery and to live on afterwards (2 Kings 4:1-7).

Who called two she bears out of the woods to kill 42 children after they had teased the man of God about being bald? Elisha disciplined these lads, which were most likely a group of rowdy boys, maybe teens (2 Kings 2:23, 24).

Who called fire down from heaven three times? Elijah called down fire from heaven three different times in two different locations (1 Kings 18:37-39) (2 Kings 1:10-12).

How many people in the Bible parted waters to get to the other side?
Moses did it with the Sea of Reeds (yam suph or the Red Sea) (Exod. 14:21, 22).
The waters stopped flowing when the Levite priests carried the Ark of the Covenant across the Jordan River (Josh. 3:14-17).
Elijah used his mantle (ornamental covering) to part and cross the Jordan (2 Kings 2:8).
Elisha took Elijah's mantle to also part and cross the Jordon River (2 Kings 2:13, 14).

How many men did the Lord kill in one night? The angel of the Lord killed one hundred and eighty five thousand men in one night (2 Kings 19:32-35). The count of the firstborn killed in Egypt is not given, but that must have been a great number of people also.

Did Yeshua use His parables to make the meanings more clear? No, some of the parables were "not" for others to understand (Luke 8:9, 10).

What was the forbidden fruit? Eve tasted the fruit from the tree of knowledge of good and evil (Gen. 2:17).

Where was Adam when Eve tasted the forbidden fruit? He was right there with her (Gen. 3:6).

Did God pronounce that Eve's pain in childbirth would be increased? It says her sorrow would be increased (Gen. 3:16). The Hebrew meaning is grief, pain, labor.

How did David's son Absalom die? When his mule went under the oak tree; his head (not his hair) got caught in the tree (probably the fork of a branch). Joab thrust three darts through Absalom's heart, ten young armor bearers surrounded and slew him. They threw him in a pit and covered him with a great heap of stones (2 Sam. 18:9-17).

Why did the woman healed from an issue with blood come trembling? According to the Torah, a woman with an issue of blood was considered ritually unclean, as well as anything she touched (Lev. 15:25-28). To touch Yeshua (a Rabbi) or anyone else would have brought severe rebuke (Luke 8:47).

Did you know nine names in the Old Testament only have two letters in them? A king named So (2 Kings 17:4) and a king named Og (Num. 21:33). A man named Ir (1 Chron. 7:12), a son named Uz (Gen. 10:23) and a son named Er (Gen. 38:3). There was a city named No (Ezek. 30:14-16), a city named On (Gen. 41:45), a city in Moab called Ar (Deut. 2:29) and a city pronounced the same way it is spelled, Ai (Josh. 7:2).

What are the shortest book and the longest book in the Bible? Shortest book: (3 John) has 299 words. Longest book: (Psalms) has 43,743 words.

What is the shortest verse and longest verse in the Bible? The shortest verse: Jesus wept (John 11:35). The longest verse: (Esther 8:9) with 90 words.

What are the shortest and longest chapters in the Bible? Longest chapter: (Psalms 119) with 176 verses. Shortest chapter: (Psalms 117) is not only the shortest, but the middle chapter in the Bible, with 594 chapters before it and after it.

Who was the son of Nimshi who drove chariots furiously? Jehu drove the chariot furiously (2 Kings 9:20). It makes you wonder if the common call of cowboys riding a bucking bronco was derived from his name and this verse, "Yahoo."

How many people in the Bible where named Dodo? There was Dodo of Issacher (Judges 10:1). There was Dodo the Alohite (2 Sam. 23:9) and Dodo of Bethlehem (2 Sam. 23:24).

How many people in the Bible where named Noah? There was Noah (Noach) and the ark. Zelophehad had five daughters; one was named Noah (Num. 26:33).

Are Adam and Tarshish the names of men or cities? There was a city named Adam (Josh. 3:16). There was a man named Tarshish (Gen. 10:4).

What accompanies increased knowledge? Knowledge increases sorrow, grief accompanies wisdom (Eccl. 1:18).

Which two women were mothers of their half-brothers, whose dad was their children's grandfather? Lot's two daughters were the women. There were two nations that started here; the Moabites and the Ammonites (Gen. 19:31-38).

Which prophet preached to dry bones? Ezekiel had the vision to preach to dry bones (Ezek. 37:1-14).

Who made the serpent on the pole and why? God told Moses to make the serpent on the pole. Anyone who was snake bitten could look at it and live (Num. 21:8, 9).

Who broke the serpent on the pole and why? Hezekiah broke the serpent on the pole. The people made it into an idol, burned incense to it and had named it Nehustan (2 Kings 18:4).

Who has more faith, a fool or a demon? The fool says there is no God (Ps. 14:1). A demon believes in God and trembles (James 2:19).

Was it a pure Jewish bloodline from King David to Yeshua? No, it was not a pure Jewish bloodline from David to Messiah (Matt. 1:3-5). The lineage listed in Matthew informs us that Tamar (Judah's daughter in law), Rahab (the harlot from Jericho) and Ruth (the Moabitess) were in the bloodline leading to Messiah.

What prophet had the dirtiest underwear? God told Jeremiah to wear a girdle and go on about a two week (which might be about a 200 mile) journey. When he got there, God told him to pull up a rock by the river bank, put his underwear under it and then return home. He was then commanded to journey back, pull it out from under the rock and he found it was profitable for nothing (Jer. 13:1-7).

After the all night east wind parted the Red Sea (Sea of Reeds), what did the Lord do to the wheels of the Egyptian chariots? The Lord probably loosened the wheels, which caused them to swerve or drag. Possibly, as the ground moistened, the wheels dragged in the mud or fell off; which would surely cause them to drive heavily (Exod. 14:21-25).

Are we still waiting (Mal. 4:5, 6) for Elijah to come? Yeshua told us that John the Baptist <u>was</u> the fulfillment of the verse in Malachi (Matt. 11:13-15) (Matt. 17:11-13) (Luke 1:17).

Has Satan ever entered a person? Satan entered into Judas (Luke 22:3) (John 13:27).

Was the day of Pentecost the first time someone was filled with the Spirit? No. People in the Old Testament had been filled with the Ruach, or the Spirit was upon them (Gen. 41:38) (Exod. 31:3) (Num. 11:25) (Jud. 14:6) (Isa. 59:21) (Ezek. 3:24). Before the day of Shavuot (Pentecost), some were also filled with the Ruach HaKodesh (Luke 1:15) (Luke 1:41) (Luke 1:67).

What New Testament events (Isa. 26:19) does "Thy dead men shall arise together with my dead body" refer to? When Yeshua died on the cross, the veil was torn in two (which revealed the Holy of Holies), the earth shook and rocks were split. Tombs opened, the bodies of saints were raised and appeared unto many in Jerusalem (Matt. 27:51-53).

How long did Mary stay with Elizabeth before John the Baptist was born? Mary stayed with Elizabeth approximately three months (Luke 1:56).

Who buried Abraham? Isaac and Ishmael buried Abraham (with Sarah) in the cave of Machpelah (Gen. 25:7-10).

What did Yeshua mean when He called the Pharisees, "ye generation of vipers"? It was John the Baptist and Yeshua who called the Pharisees "ye generation of vipers." A better rendering would be "offspring of the serpent" (Young's Concordance) (Matt. 12:34) (Matt. 3:7) (Matt. 23:33) (Luke 3:7).

How many times did the cock crow when Peter denied Yeshua? The cock did not crow three times, but it was Peter who would deny knowing the Lord three times (Matt. 26:74) (Mark 14:72) (Luke 22:60) (John 18:27). In Mark's account, the cock immediately crows a second time, but the three denials occurred before any crowing took place (Mark 14:68-72). The other writers just say the cock crowed. Yeshua had predicted Peter would deny Him three times "before" the cock crows (Matt. 26:34) (Mark 14:30) (Luke 22:34) (John 13:38).

Give the Old Testament verse stating the sale price for Yeshua when Judas betrayed him. (Zechariah 11:12, 13) was fulfilled in: (Matt. 26:15) (Mark 14:10, 11) (Luke 22:3-6).

Give the Old Testament verse foretelling Yeshua riding the foal of a donkey. (Zechariah 9:9) was fulfilled in: (Matt. 21:2-9) (Mark 11:2-10) (Luke 19:30-40) (John 12:13-16).

Give the Old Testament verse foretelling John the Baptist preparing a highway for Messiah (our God). Compare the terminology that is used about God in (Isa. 40:3) and (Matt. 3:3) (Mark 1:2-4) (Luke 1:76) (John 1:23).

Give the Old Testament verses about Yeshua's hands and feet being pierced and lots cast for his garment. The verses in (Ps. 22:16-18) were fulfilled in: (Matt. 27:35) (Mark 15:24) (Luke 23:33, 34) (John 19:23, 24).

Give the Old Testament verses that Yeshua was quoting when he drove the moneychangers out of the temple with a cord (Matt. 21:13) (Mark 11:17) (Luke 19:46). (Isa. 56:7) and (Jer. 7:11) first mention "house of prayer" and "den of thieves."

How did the disciples know (Luke 22:10) which man to meet and arrange a room for the last supper (Passover)? In their culture, it was unusual to see "a man" carrying water. This was normally done by women. Yeshua instructed the disciples to find such a man in town and follow him to his home. If lots of men were carrying water, it would have been difficult to pick the correct one out of a crowd.

How many men did Gideon begin with to go against the Midianites? How many ended up going? He started with 32,000 men. The Lord thought that was too many and ended up whittling it down to 300 (Judges 7:3, 7).

What is the hire/wages (Deut. 23:18) of a dog? A female prostitute in this verse is called a whore. The male counterpart is called a "dog" because of the manner in which he copulates. The Lord did not want the wages from prostitution in His Temple.

How are God's people destroyed? My people are destroyed for lack of knowledge (Hosea 4:6).

How many people were present for the "last supper"? What is now called the "last supper" was actually the Passover meal. When Yeshua said someone would betray Him, one asked, "is it I?" Then another asked, "is it I?" His reply, "No, it is one of the twelve" (Mark 14:19, 20). That is at least 15 people.

Do you know which verses these current day expressions were derived from?
By the skin of my teeth (Job 19:20).
In God we trust (Ps. 56:11).
On the wings of a dove (Ps. 68:13).
A little birdie told me (Eccl. 10:20).
Holier than thou (Isa. 65:5).
Read the handwriting on the wall (Dan. 5:17).
Weighed in the balances and found wanting (Dan. 5:27).

Why did the Pharisees (Luke 19:39, 40) Yeshua to rebuke his disciples? The disciples were giving Yeshua praise due only to YHVH, God of Israel. Yeshua responded, if He quieted the disciples, the stones would cry out who He was (Hab. 2:11).

Can you give 2 verses that say who every knee shall bow to? Every knee shall bow to YHVH, God of Israel (Isa. 45:23). Every knee shall bow to Yeshua the Messiah (Phil. 2:10, 11). Recognizing Messiah as God and Lord is giving glory to God.

How many verses in the Old Testament say who the Saviour is? Here are a few: (Ps. 106:21) (Isa. 43:3-11) (Isa. 45:15-22) (Isa. 49:26) (Jer.14:7, 8) (Hos. 13:4). Did you notice how interchangeable these verses are about the identity of our Saviour? (Eph. 3:23) (Titus 1:3, 4) (Titus 2:10, 13) (Titus 3:4, 6)

Are "Spirit of Jesus and Holy Spirit" used interchangeably? (Acts 16:7) (Rom. 8:9) (Phil. 1:19) (1 Peter 1:11)

Why are the genealogies in Matthew and Luke so different? In Matthew, Joseph's bloodline goes through King Solomon in the tribe of Judah (Matt. 1:6). In Luke, the lineage follows Mary back to the prophet Nathan, also King David's son in the tribe of Judah (Luke 3:31). Both prove bloodline and legal parenthood.

Who, with his people, repaired a wall with a weapon in one hand and a tool in the other? Nehemiah and his people rebuilt the wall (Neh. 4:16-18).

Why is the word "Easter" in the King James Bible? It is actually the Greek word "pascha," which means Passover (Acts 12:4). In the time of King James (1611), the translators considered the three events spring, Easter and Passover interchangeably associated together. They used the word "Easter" to convey that it was spring time. Different Bible translations do use the word Passover (Hebrew-Pesach).

When did the last miracle associated with Elisha occur? A dead man was thrown into Elisha's tomb. When his dead body hit Elisha's bones, he came back to life (2 Kings 13:21).

Who or what is Mystery Babylon, (Rev. 17:5) the Mother of harlots? There is usually one city referred to in history that sits on seven hills (Rev. 17:9). Rome is the city that houses the revised Babylon false worship system of spiritual impurity.

Are the "garlands" in the book of Acts the same as on our Christmas tree? No, the garlands of the priests of Jupiter (Zeus) were more like a wreath or a chaplet (Acts 14:13).

How many biblical people did not eat for 40 days? Moses did not eat for 40 days (Deut. 9: 18). The food nourished Elijah for 40 days (1 Kings 19:8). We know Yeshua fasted for 40 days (Luke 4:2).

What unusual cargo did Solomon's ships bring from Tarshish every three years? The ships brought gold, silver, ivory, apes and peacocks (2 Chron. 9:21).

Who is Capernaum named for? It is the "town of Nahum" (Kaphar-Nahum).

Give three verses containing the name Emmanuel. What does it mean? (Isa. 7:14) (Isa. 8:8) (Matt. 1:23) Emmanuel means "with us is YHVH."

Who were the only people to give a sacrifice on a ship? After tossing Jonah overboard, the waters became calm and the men feared the Lord exceedingly. They offered a sacrifice and made vows (Jonah 1:15, 16).

Who are the only four people to commit suicide in the Old Testament? Samson knew he would drop the temple on himself as well as the enemy. He killed more enemies in his death than he did during his life (Judges 16:28-30). Saul fell on his sword (1 Sam. 31:4). Saul's armor bearer fell on his sword (1 Sam. 31:5). Bathsheba's grandfather Ahithophel went home and hung himself (2 Sam. 17:23).

Who is the only person to commit suicide in the New Testament? Judas hung himself (Matt. 27:5).

Who raised Yeshua from the dead? It says God raised Yeshua from the dead (Acts 2:32). Yeshua said he would raise His own body from the dead (John 2:19-21).

Where in the Bible is the term, "God the Father, God the Son, God the Holy Spirit"? This statement does not appear in this form anywhere in the Bible, nor does just "God the Son."

Where in the gospels did Yeshua say, "It is more blessed to give than to receive"? This statement is not found in the gospels. We know these as the words of Yeshua because Paul quoted them (Acts 20:35).

Where in the Bible is the verse, "Do unto others as you would have them do unto you"? It is not in the Bible. It is the Golden Rule.

From what Greek poetry was Paul quoting, "As certain as your poets said"? The verse says, "For in Him we live and move and have our being, as certain of your own poets have said, for we are also His offspring." Paul was in Greece and quoted their poets to make his point while he spoke on Mars Hill (Acts 17:28). The phrase came from the "Phaenomena of Aratus," and is found in the "Hymn to Zeus of Cleanthes."

Who was Paul quoting, (1 Cor. 15:33) "Evil communications corrupt good manners"? An Athenian dramatist by the name of Menander (342-291 BC) said, "It must be that evil communications corrupt good manners." This saying, though not in the Bible, had become a proverbial figure of speech and was used by Paul.

What Cretian prophet (Titus 1:12) was Paul quoting? In the 6th century BC, Epimenidas (a Cretian prophet) said, "The Creatians are always liars, evil beasts and slow bellies." Paul was quoting this when writing to Titus.

What book in the Bible has the verse, "God helps him who helps himself"? This is not a verse found in the Bible. It is just a common saying. In 1698, Algernon Sidney wrote, "God helps those who help themselves." In 1733 Ben Franklin wrote, "God helps him who helps himself."

Where does the Bible say that cleanliness is next to godliness? This phrase is not found in the Bible. We know this quote from a sermon in 1740, by John Wesley. His precise words were, "Clean is indeed next to godliness." This quote may even go back some 2,000 years to Phinehas ben Yair.

Where in the Bible is the saying, "When in Rome, do as Romans do"? This saying is not biblical either. Paul said, "I am made all things to all men that I might by all means save some" (1 Cor. 9:22). This may be where the saying originated.

Where in the Bible is the saying, "God works in mysterious ways, His wonders to perform"? This quote is not biblical either; though the Lord may often work in ways that are mysterious to us. These words came from a poem by William Cowper (1731-1800).

Where in the Bible is the saying, "Each generation will grow wiser and weaker"? This phrase is not in the Bible and its source is unknown, but it may have come from Walter Pope (1630-1714), "May I govern my passion with an absolute sway and grow wiser and better as my strength wears away."

How many garments did Samson pay on his gambling debt? How did he get these garments? Samson killed 30 men and took the likely bloody garments to insultingly pay the ones who dishonestly used Delilah to solve his riddle (Judges 14:19). They may have recognized who the garments had belonged to!

What were Shadrach, Meshach and Abednego's real Hebrew names? (Shadrach – Hananiah) (Meshach – Michael) (Abednego – Azariah) Their names were changed by the Babylonians (Dan. 1:7).

Why were the Hebrew boys names changed? After conquering a people, the traditional trend was to kill the men, enslave (and sometimes castrate) the young men and change their names to wipe out their culture, and impregnate the women to eliminate the heritage and bloodline.

What was the penalty for speaking against the God of Shadrach, Meshach and Abednego? They shall be cut in pieces and their houses shall be made a dung hill (Dan. 3:29).

Are believers instructed to hate anything? We are allowed to hate that which is evil (Rom. 12:9). God does too (Heb. 1:9).

Why was it risky for 276 people to sail? The Romans considered sailing after mid-Sept. to early Oct. as doubtful, and after mid-Nov. as suicidal. Sailing was dangerous because the fast (Day of Atonement) was already past (Acts 27:9-12, 37).

Why were twin gods' names on the ship? In mythology, Castor and Pollux were called patrons of sailors (Acts 28:11).

Did Herod and Jezebel live up to what their names meant? Herod is the root from where we get the word "hero," and though she was spiritually impure, the name Jezebel means "chaste."

How much hair did Absalom grow and cut off every year? Absalom grew nearly five pounds or 2.3 kilograms of hair each year (2 Sam. 14:26).

Did the angel Michael fight the prince of Persia 21 days before coming to answer Daniel's prayer? The answer is no. Michael did not fight the Prince of Persia for 21 days, nor did Michael come to answer Daniel's prayer. The angel who had withstood the prince of Persia for 21 days (the one Michael had come to help) was the angel who was now talking to Daniel (Dan. 10:13-15).

Who lured Baal worshippers together and had them slain, then did not walk in God's law? Jehu lured Baal worshippers to one place and had them slain (2 Kings 10:18-28). Then Jehu failed to walk in the ways of the Lord (2 Kings 10:31).

What was the first word in the first sermon that Yeshua gave? The first word was, "Repent" (Matt. 4:17).

Who is the True God? Our King (Jer. 10:10) and our True God (1 John 5:20) is Yeshua the Messiah. Messiah is the image or representation of the invisible God (YHVH) (Col. 1:15).

How long was Yeshua in the heart of the earth? As predicted, Yeshua was in the heart of the earth for three days and three nights (Matt. 12:40).

Who held the clothes while Stephen was being stoned? It was Paul (Acts 7:58).

Why were they stoning Stephen? They were stoning Stephen because he had stated Yeshua the Messiah was the power and presentation of the God of Moses (Acts 7:53-57). Only YHVH can receive our spirit, so by calling Yeshua "Lord," Stephen implied to those listening that Messiah was God (Vs. 59). The right hand was associated with YHVH (Exod. 15:6) (Ps. 118:16).

How scared was Belshazzar when the hand wrote on the wall? His knees smote one against another (Dan. 5:6).

What would Joab have paid for someone to have killed Absalom? He would have paid ten shekels of silver and a girdle (2 Sam. 18:11).

What were the Scriptures (Acts 17:11) that the Bereans were searching daily? He spoke of the "Tanakh," (Gen.-Mal.) or what we call the Old Testament, which contains the Torah. Paul said it was good for reproof, instruction, etc. (2 Tim 3:16). The Brit Chadashah, or New Testament, did not exist at that time.

Did only Jewish authors write the Bible? No, there is a section in the book of Daniel that king Nebuchadnezzar wrote after seven years of his living like a wild beast (Dan. 4:34-37).

What were the only five animals used as acceptable sacrifices in the Bible? They were sheep, goats, cattle (oxen), pigeons and doves.

How did they know (1 Kings 1:1-4) King David was dying? They covered him, but he put off no heat. They searched the whole kingdom to find a maiden (named Abishag) who lay with him, but he "knew" her not.

Did Yeshua sweat blood when praying in the garden? Yes, the mixing of sweat and blood is from extreme straining, often associated with childbirth. This condition is now called Hematidrosis (Luke 22:44).

Martin Luther nailed how many points, to what door, when? It was 95 points of contention against Rome's teachings that were contrary to the Bible. He nailed it to the door of All Saints Church on October 31, 1517.

How many people traveled with Yeshua and the disciples? There were the seventy (Luke 10:17). There were the "other" seventy (Luke 10:1). By adding the disciples, it would make over 150 people traveling with the Lord.

What is the oldest profession mentioned in Scripture? No, the answer is not prostitution. After Adam and Eve sinned and realized they were naked, they "sewed" fig leaves together to cover themselves (Gen. 3:7). Sewing could be the oldest profession mentioned, unless farming and shepherding came first.

Name three things in the Ark of the Covenant? The Ten Commandments, a bowl of manna and Aaron's rod that budded were in the Ark. These are symbolic of the Torah, our daily Bread and resurrection from the dead.

How many stripes did Yeshua receive? It does not say how many stripes the Lord took. It was Paul that took forty save one, five times (2 Cor. 11:24). This is often mistakenly attributed to the Lord.

What is the correct chronological order of Paul's thirteen letters that were written over a twenty year span? Many scholars say the earliest letter written was Galatians; 1 Thess.; 2 Thess.; 1 Cor.; 2 Cor.; Romans; Colossians; Philemon; Ephesians; Philippians; 1 Timothy; Titus; and last was 2 Timothy.

Why are the Catholic Ten Commandments different from the Protestant Ten Commandments? The Papacy combined the first and the second Commandment as one. Then, they split the tenth Commandment about coveting into two separate commands, to make up the gap of the now missing one. This was done to take attention away from the fact that we are not to make, use or have any graven images, idols or relics. Nor should we incorporate them into our worship. Now, the Catholics have two commandments about coveting, #9 and #10.

Who made the Ten Commandments? God carved out and wrote the first set of tablets (Ex. 31:18) (Ex. 32:15, 16). God wrote the second set of tablets also, but made Moses carve out the second set of tablet stones (Ex. 34:1, 4).

How long after his conversion did Paul meet with any of the disciples? Paul had gone to preach to Gentiles for three years before he met with two of the disciples (Gal. 2:15-19).

Do Islamists claim to be descendants of Ishmael? Yes, they are originally half Egyptian (Hagar) and half Jewish (Abram). That means they use the Jewish Scriptures to document their claim of heritage to Ishmael and Abram, but in other situations, they try to discredit the same Jewish Scripture as unreliable!

Other than the biblical record, is there any other evidence King David ever existed? A dig in Tel Dan in Aug. 1993, uncovered a tablet with the specific Hebrew writing "house of David" engraved on it.

What happened when the scribes, chief priests, elders, Temple guards and armed crowd asked the Lord if He was Yeshua of Nazareth? The Lord said "I Am," and they all fell down. They had to get up to finish arresting Him (John 18:6).

Why is Zedekiah's downfall predicted in 2 different books? It is predicted in two books (Jer. 32:4, 5) (Ezek. 12:13). The fulfillment is revealed in three different places (2 Ki. 25:6, 7) (Jer. 10: 10, 11) (Jer. 39:6, 7).

Is (Luke 18:24-27), "camel through the eye of a needle," a reference to a needle gate into the city? He was not speaking of a "needle gate" into the city. Whether He meant hawser or camel, the listening fishermen knew it would be difficult to put either through their net mending needles. Recent teachings since the 9th century say, if you arrived late after the huge city gates were closed, you'd have to unpack your camel, pull it through an oval opening in the city wall (the needle gate), and reload it once inside. Once inside, you'd be overseen by soldiers, in case an enemy would try to use this gate as an entry point. Although this teaching makes sense, the needle gate has never been verified by any biblical, historical, or archeological evidence; nor has it been documented by any reliable source.

What was one of the differences between Jewish and Samaritan worship? The Samaritan woman told the Lord that her forefathers worshiped on this mountain, "yet you (Jews) say Jerusalem is where men should worship" (John 4:20). The Samaritans believed the command for Moses to build an altar for worship on Mount Ebal was still valid (Deut. 27:4, 5). Even Joshua had built an altar on Mount Ebal, as Moses previously had (Josh. 8:30, 31). The Samaritans had not accepted the Temple in Jerusalem as the place to worship like the Israelites had. Samaritans were still worshiping at the same location Moses had, many years before.

How many stones did it take to kill Goliath? The stone did not kill him, but knocked him down as David predicted. He took Goliath's sword and cut off his head (1 Sam. 17:46-51). David carried Goliath's head all the way to Jerusalem. Some speculate the other four stones were for the other four giants later slain by David and his men (possibly Goliath's brothers or cousins). One of these giants had six fingers and six toes on each hand and foot (2 Sam. 21:16-22) (I Chron. 20:4-8).

Were there millions of years between each day of creation as some Christian evolutionists try to portray? The third day, God put vegetation, plants and fruit trees on the earth (Gen. 1:9-13). It was the fourth day when God put the greater and lesser lights in the heavens (Gen. 1:14-19). If there were millions of years in between each day of creation, how would the vegetation have lived, pollinated and reproduced for millions of years without light?

What root word do "exit, export and odometer" come from? The root word is Exodus. The (ex) means "leaving," as in exit and export. The (od) means "proceeding," like the mileage on the odometer.

Is the term "helpmate" used for Eve in the Bible? No, the Bible does not say helpmate. It says "help meet," which means a suitable helper (Gen. 2:18, 20). This is not what the word "mate" means today.

Is Eden the name of a land or a man? (Not counting the Garden in Eden) The king of Tyre traded with the land of Eden (Ezek. 27:23). A man was named Eden (2 Chron. 29:12).

What is the Pentateuch? This would more accurately be called the Torah (Law of Moses). It is the first five books of the Bible; Genesis, Exodus, Leviticus, Numbers and Deuteronomy. Why do we need to follow Rome, and call it something else?

What verse in the Bible have you never, ever, ever heard a preacher use in a sermon? The verse you probably never hear used as a lesson in church is (Ezek. 23:20).

Name any descendants of Daniel, Shadrach, Meshach or Abednego. You probably won't find any, due to the fact they were eunuchs (Dan. 1:3-18).

What did the prophet Nathan predict would be done to humiliate King David openly for what he had done in secret? Nathan predicted an adversary from in his own house would openly lie with David's wives (2 Sam. 12:11, 12). They pitched a tent on the rooftop and Absalom went in to his father's concubines in the sight of Israel (2 Sam. 16:22). This was likely the same rooftop that David's lust for Bathsheba began.

Why did Ahithophel give Absalom the advice (2 Sam. 16:21) to humiliate David by lying with his wives? Ahithophel was the father of Eliam (2 Sam. 23:24). This made him the grandfather of Bathsheba (2 Sam. 11:3). He was most likely attempting to avenge his granddaughter's adultery and murder of her husband Uriah, formerly orchestrated by David.

When was (Joel 2:28) fulfilled? On the day of the feast of Shavuot (Pentecost), Peter stated this was what the prophet Joel spoke of (Acts 2:16-21).

Why is September (meaning seven) our 9th month, October (meaning eight) our 10th month, November (meaning nine) our 11th month and December (meaning ten) our 12th month? Because, when the months of July and August were designated to honor Julius and Augustus Caesars, they weren't added to the end of the established calendar. They inserted the new months into the middle of the existing calendar, which pushed the others two months ahead.

Were the Romans or the Jews responsible for killing Yeshua? Even though the Lord laid down His life and they could do nothing outside the plan of God, the chief priests inspected, bound and delivered the perfect sacrificial Lamb. The Romans (Gentiles) actually performed the high priest's duty of shedding of the sacrificial blood of the Lamb. The Gentiles also took an active part in the final sacrifice and both Jew and Gentile witnessed the resurrection as well.

With Whom did Jacob wrestle all night? Jacob wrestled the Lord (Gen. 32:24, 30).

Who fell out a window and died when Paul preached late into the night? Eutychus fell asleep, dropped out a third story window and died. Paul laid himself on the lad and restored his life (Acts 20:7-12).

How many times is the word "piss" in the King James Bible? Believe it or not, the word is there a total of seven times (1 Sam. 25:22) (1 Kings 14:10; 16:11; 21:21) (2 Kings 9:8; 18:27) (Isa. 36:12).

Did Lot's wife really get turned into a pillar of salt? Not only did Josephus travel to see Lot's wife after the time of Messiah, but Irenaeus and Clement of Rome also testified to seeing this pillar of salt. They even comment how amazing it was, that all her members were still intact after so much time (Antiquities of the Jews, Book 1, 11:4 and Footnotes).

Who were Pharaoh's magicians, (Exod. 7:9-12, 22) whose rods became snakes and (Exod. 8:7, 18) who duplicated a couple of Moses' first plagues? Jannes and Jambres were two of Pharaoh's magicians (2 Tim. 3:8).

Was Paul's thorn in the flesh an eye/vision problem? There is a reference about someone who cared so much for Paul; he felt they would have given him their eyes if they could have (Gal. 4:15). Paul also makes a comment about the large letters he is writing with his own hand, as if they knew he didn't see well (Gal. 6:11). Paul also mentions a "messenger of Satan" sent to buffet him. Was this an eye problem or an inflated ego, because of the exaltation Paul would often receive for his abundance of revelations? Was his appearance so scarred from beatings, stoning and scourging that he was hard to look at? It seems to me that Paul was surprised he had to pray more than once (he said three times) for it to be removed, and it wasn't. Then he resigned himself to the fact he was going to have to live with it. He did not assemble a team of prayer warriors to pray for years until it was finally removed, he just dealt with it.

Were Joseph and Yeshua carpenters? Joseph may have been an engraver or artificer (skilled craftsman/manual occupation). The text calls Messiah (a rabbi) "the carpenter's son."

Why do some Bibles say (2 Sam. 6:23) that David's wife Michal had no children? Then, it says Michal had five sons (2 Sam. 21:8) and the father was Adriel? The footnotes in your study Bible will relay that it should read "Merab" had five sons. I don't know why they didn't just put that in the verse. It says that Merab, who is Michal's older sister, was married to Adriel (1 Sam. 18:19).

Were Adam and Eve in the Garden of Eden? The garden was "in" the land of Eden (Gen. 2:8).

Does God ever send an evil spirit upon a man? The Lord sent an evil spirit upon Saul (1 Sam. 16:14) (1 Sam. 18:10). Even Saul's servants were aware of the evil spirit from God that troubled him (1 Sam. 16:15). The Hebrew word "ra" (evil) can also simply mean bad. The Lord did allow Job to be tested by an "evil" spirit sent from God, so we may expect to be tested as well.

Did Moses part and close the "Red sea"? If you check your concordance, the Hebrew actually says "yam suph," which means sea of reeds (rushes) (Exod. 10:10). There are about 23 verses using this particular name. The word can apply to a great body of water, like a sea or even a lake that can be miles across. Because of the specific name, it was most likely a large lake that got parted and not a saltwater sea. These reeds do not grow in saltwater. Everything in the story still happened; does it matter if it was fresh or saltwater?

When the Israelites grumbled for the food they longed for back in Egypt, how much "quail" did the Lord send? It says the quail were two cubits (three feet) deep, a day's journey in any direction (Num. 11:31). They gathered ten homers (60 bushels) apiece (Verse 32). The grumbling people were struck with a plague while still chewing the meat and were buried at Kibroth Hattaavah (Verses 33, 34).

Who does the prophet Micah say will be born in Bethlehem? This is a great point foretelling and identifying the Messiah (Micah 5:2). The Ruler in Israel to be born in Bethlehem (Messiah), whose goings forth are from old (before time) and from age everlasting (indefinite time). The Messiah is none other than YHVH, the Lord God of Israel.

How many people traveled in the wilderness for 40 years? According to a census counting the populations of the 12 tribes before and after the 40 years; they started with a total of 603,550 men over 20 and finished with 601,730 men. This count seemingly did not include women and children (Exod. 12:37). The population of some of the tribes increased while others decreased, and some remained close to the same. Don't forget about the mixed multitude of many non-Israelites who went with them also (Exod. 12:38). There could have easily been over a million people involved.

What is the difference between wine and strong drink? They would add about 20% wine to the normal drinking water to purify it. They could drink it without major intoxication. Strong drink was undiluted straight wine (fermented) and did cause intoxication and societal problems, but was still only wine. The art of distilling, which produces grain alcohols like whiskey, vodka and gin; was not invented until about 300 years after Messiah's visit.

What did Thomas say (John 20:28) when he touched the holes in Messiah's hands and side? He responded, "My Lord and my God" (my Kurios and my Theos). This statement by Thomas contains words and terms that could only be used for YHVH, the Lord God of Israel. Any other application would be blasphemy, yet the Lord approved of his answer.

When the Lord returns, will the Mount of Olives be the first place on earth His feet touch? If He is supposed to come back to where He left from, it says He walked with them as far as Bethany and then ascended (Luke 24:50, 51).

What woman's age & burial is in Scripture? Sarah (Gen. 23).

Did God and Abram make a blood covenant together? No, Abram did not participate in this covenant. Two people walking through the middle of the severed animals would signify that whoever breaks the agreement should also be cut in half. While Abram slept; only the Lord passed through the middle of the halved animals (Gen. 15:10-18). Could Abram ever break this agreement made by the Lord alone? Abram's circumcision would have been his blood covenant.

What two men lied about their wives being their sisters? Abraham and Isaac lied to Abimelech (Gen. 20:2, 26:7). If this was the same Abimelech of Gerar that they both lied to; I can imagine him thinking, "If one more person tells me his wife is his sister, I'll have his head on a platter!"

Why do some Bibles say (John 5:4) an angel stirred the waters of Bethesda and some Bibles omit this verse? The oldest manuscripts, including what Jerome used in 405 AD, do not have this verse in them. It was added to later manuscripts and John did not write it. But, the common understanding was, that it was God's power stirring the water (John 5:7).

What is the last verse in the book of Mark? The last verse is (Mark 16:8). The oldest manuscripts do not have (verses 9-20), which were added centuries later and Mark did not write them.

With what words (Matt. 6:13) does the Lord's Prayer finish? It ends with "deliver us from evil." The last statement, "For Thine is the Kingdom, the power, the glory, etc." was added to later manuscripts. Matthew did not write it. See (Luke 11:2-4).

Who said, "Let him who is without sin, cast the first stone"? Don't you wonder where the man was, who was also caught in the act? The Torah said he was an equally guilty participant. It turns out John did not write this story at all; it was added by someone else centuries later (John 8:1-11).

Was the verse (1 John 5:7) in the oldest manuscripts? No, this was not in the oldest manuscripts, it was added centuries later, and John did not write this verse either.

Why were Joseph's brothers amazed at the seating for dinner? They were surprised because the Egyptian strangers had known to arrange their seating in order from the oldest to the youngest brothers (Gen. 43:33).

Did they only eat bread and drink wine at the last supper? We mistakenly call it "the last supper" or communion, but they were celebrating His last "Passover meal" (Exod. 12:1-14). This consisted of roast lamb, bitter herbs, unleavened bread and wine. The bread was similar to a big saltine cracker. Anyway, He ate suppers after He rose from the dead too! It seemed weird to me when a church served us yeast raised, icing covered, sliced pastry for communion. The thin round wafers with "IHS" stamped on it have a similarity to Babylon sun god worship (round cakes to queen of heaven). Rome's influence has distorted communion into an unbiblical ritualistic liturgy.

When distributing bread at the Passover, did the Lord say, "this is my body which is broken for you"? He did not say, "broken;" (Luke 22:19) He said "given." It says "not a bone of Him shall be broken" (Exod. 12:46) (Ps. 34:20) (John. 19:36).

Was Rahab's service to Israel a spur of the moment decision? She may have pondered about YHVH for decades, because she said the whole city heard about God delivering the Israelites from Egypt forty years earlier (Josh. 2:8-11).

What was one of the most unusual public executions in the wilderness? When Korah, Dathan and Abiram rose up in opposition to Moses, the earth opened up and swallowed them. Then the fire consumed the 250 men (Num. 16:28-35).

Is there any association between the woman who was sick for twelve years and the twelve year old dying daughter? There is no mention of these two being related. The number twelve is for governmental perfection/union of the people with God; which, in this case may symbolically mean Messiah came to heal the sick and raise the "spiritually dead" in the 12 tribes of Israel (Matt. 9:18-26). There are also 12 loaves of showbread and 12 stones in the priest's breastplate.

Was Jezebel a sexually immoral woman? There is no mention of her being unchaste. She was the king's wife; nobody would have dared approach her improperly. The slight association with questionable behavior may stem from past generations, where ladies of the evening would put on make-up or "paint their faces" and then sit in the window to solicit clients (2 Kings 9:30). But wait, she did not paint her "face"; it says she painted her "eyes." This has nothing to do with lipstick or make-up as we know it today. She was "spiritually impure" because of her endorsing the Baal worship and causing the slaughter of the Levite priests (1 Kings 18:13) (2 Kings 9:22).

What was Joseph's cup that was hidden in Benjamin's saddle bags used for? Joseph used the cup for divination (Gen. 44:5, 15).

Why was Benjamin of such interest to Joseph? Benjamin and Joseph were the only brothers from the same mother, Rachel (Gen. 43:29).

Is there a difference between the "body" of Christ and the "bride" of Christ, (Rev. 21:2, 9, 12, 14) the New Jerusalem? We know Israel is called the bride or wife in the Old Testament and the New Testament church is called His body. It seems His body, which He made ready, will be presented to Him for a bride (Eph. 5:27). The church is combined with His Old Testament believers to be His bride (Eph. 2:14, 3:6). This would make the New Jerusalem a symbolic description of His believers from all time, but let's not rule out the possibility of it being a literal city.

Why would the Lord put dirt and spit in the blind man's eyes? This seems rather tongue in cheek. From dust were we created and to dust shall we return. God caused a mist to water the earth, then added dust to create Adam (Gen. 2:6, 7). If God can create us from dust and moisture, surely He can heal us with it too (John 9:6).

Which prophet is twice associated with horses and chariots of fire? The prophet is Elisha (2 Kings 2:11) (2 Kings 6:17).

Do you know how many verses in the Bible were written in Aramaic? Out of over 23,000 verses, it seems only about 250 were written in Aramaic (Gen. 31:47) (Ezra 4:8-6:18; 7:12-26) (Job 36:2) (Jer. 10:11) (Dan. 2:4-7:28).

How many children did Abraham have? Ishmael and Isaac, then after Sarah died, Abraham got married again and had about six more children (Gen. 25:1, 2).

Where was Abraham from? He was a Babylonian from Ur of the Chaldeans, a town near Babylon (Gen. 11:31). Salem was a pagan city and didn't become Jerusalem until centuries later.

Were there circumcisions in the wilderness? It appears that they did not circumcise while in the wilderness, because they had a group ceremony after crossing the Jordan (Josh. 5:1-8).

Were Solomon and Herod's Temple burned on the same day? Yes, we find Jeremiah (586 BC) (Jer. 52:12, 13) and Josephus (70 AD) both mention the tenth day of the fifth month (War of the Jews, book 6, 4:5). There are other bad things that have taken place in history on the ninth of Av, which is like a Jewish Friday the thirteenth.

Why did Yeshua wait four days to raise Lazarus from the dead? There was a teaching at the time, perhaps from the Sadducees; the spirit didn't leave a body until the third day after death. Yeshua waited until the fourth day to show them He had power over life and death (John 11:39-43).

Did angels (Gen. 6:2-4) ever mate with humans to create giants? No, there is nothing in the Bible about angels or spirit beings mating with mankind.

How long did it take (Job 42:10) for Job to receive double? God restored and doubled Job's wealth over the course of time. The animals needed time to reproduce and increase in number. But why did Job only have seven more sons and three more daughters? Adding ten more children to the ten that were lost is still double.

Were the actual continents divided (Gen. 10:26) back in the days of Peleg? This was several generations after the flood. There is no record from any civilization in the past 4,000 years that reports huge land masses moving thousands of miles away from each other. Peleg, whose name in Hebrew signifies division, was born at the time of the dispersion of the nations to several countries (Antiquities of the Jews, book one, 6:4). A couple thousand years ago, it seems they didn't think of the "days of Peleg" as continents dividing.

Where does it say, "A virgin shall conceive"? Most people would answer (Isa. 7:14) and (Matt. 1:23). It is by translation that we get the word "virgin." The Hebrew word implies chastity, but simply means "young woman." It is by Mary's response to the angel, "how can this be? For I have not known man," that we also know of her chastity (Luke 1:24).

Did Messiah talk about hell three times more than He talked about heaven? If we count the references the Lord made about hell; there are about sixteen in the whole New Testament. But, before the end of the book of Matthew, there are about fifty references with the word "heaven."

When did Methuselah die? His name means (when he dies-judgment or when he is dead-it will come). Methuselah begat Lamech at 187; and Lamech begat Noah at 182 (Gen. 5:22, 28). If Methuselah was 369 years old when Noah was born and the flood came when Noah was 600; that is 969 years (Gen. 7:6).

Are we still waiting for the Gospel to be preached unto the entire world? Paul seemed to think he was seeing the fulfillment of prophecy from (Ps. 19:4). The Gospel was going out to the entire world, present and continuing (Rom. 10:18).

Why does God (Job 38:31) mention the constellations Pleiades and Orion? Pleiades and Orion are recently defined as gravitationally connected star clusters. The Hebrew "binds Pleiades" means tie or join; and "bands/cords" of Orion means drag or draw together. It was understood long ago that God was the designing power holding all of creation in place.

Was Paul a member of the Sanhedrin? Paul was authorized to go from house to house arresting believers, (Acts 8:3) not only in Jerusalem, but in Damascus and other cities too (Acts 22:3-5). He even claimed to have been a Pharisee (Phil. 3:5). If Paul was not an actual member of the Sanhedrin, would they have allowed him to vote (Acts 26:9-12) in their elite councils?

How long were Noah and his family on the ark before it rained? Who shut the door? After the Lord shut them in, they waited seven days (Gen. 7:10, 16).

Is (Exodus 6:2, 3) a contradiction? Since it is common knowledge that Abram referred to God as Yahveh (YHVH), verse 3 only makes sense if phrased as a question. "And by the name YHVH, did I not make Myself known to them?"

What is the meaning of selah and amen? Selah carries the meaning of "think about it," and amen is more like "so be it."

What is the difference between "prophecy and prophesy"? "Prophecy" is divine prediction of future events; and "prophesy" is inspired speaking. He prophesied a prophecy.

Did Mary Magdalene pour the spikenard on Messiah? No. Six days before Passover, at Lazarus and Martha's house, their sister Mary anointed His feet (John 12:1-3). Two days before Passover, at Simon the leper's house, an unidentified woman anointed His head (Matt. 26:6) (Mark 14:3). Both events drew criticism from onlookers.

On the cross, why did Messiah say, "My God, my God, why have you forsaken me?" He was referencing the whole of Psalms 22 and following chapters; which contain the prediction of the piercing of His hands and feet, and casting lots over His robe, now fulfilled! These passages conclude with confidence, a context of faith, hope and expectation for deliverance and victory; not only for Israel, but the nations (Gentiles) also.

After the woman at the well, how long did Messiah stay with the Samaritans? He stayed with them two days (John 4:39-42).

What did Messiah mean by "taking up your cross daily and following Him?" The word "cross" translates from "stauros," meaning stake (Matt. 10:37-39). This is not an instruction to carry an instrument of death on our backs (Matt. 16:24, 25). This reminds us of both Abraham and the Israelites, always being ready to pull up their tent stake/pole daily and go wherever the Lord may lead them (Mark 8:34, 35). We should be willing to take up our stake, forsake this world, even mother and father; set aside self-interest, and go where He may direct; resulting in eternal life (Luke 9:23-27). Being crucified in our place; taking up your stake is more about living for Him daily, not dying.

Were there any women rulers in Israel or Judah? Deborah ruled for forty years (Judges 4:4 thru 5:32). Athaliah ruled for six years (2 Chron. 22:10-12).

Who did Isaiah predict would release Israel after the seventy year captivity? King Cyrus admired the divine power identifying him in the prophecy written over 100 years previous (Isa. 44:28; 45:1-6, 13), and let the Jews (536 BC) return to Jerusalem (Ezra 6:3-5). To avoid forfeiting their accumulated wealth, some remained in Babylon. It is said, only 42,462 Jews returned to Israel (Antiquities of the Jews; book 11, 1:1-3).

Who told Ezra to rebuild the Temple and Jerusalem? It was King Artaxerxes Longimanus (458 BC) who decreed and funded the restoration to Jerusalem and the Temple (Ezra 7:11-26). This would likely be the starting point for the prophetic 490 years from (Dan. 9:24-27).

Who told Nehemiah to rebuild the wall? It was King (445 BC) Artaxerxes Longimanus who decreed the repair to the walls and gates (Neh. 2:6-8). This king is reputed to have had one or both arms so long that when standing, he could touch his knees or below. (Library of Biblical Literature 1856, Vol. 4, London) (Critical and Popular Bible Encyclopedia 1901, pg. 162, Howard Severance)

How did Sisera die? Jael drove a tent stake through his head and nailed him to the ground (Judges 4:21).

What was the symbolism (Exod. 28:33, 34; 39:24-26) of the pomegranates on the hem of the priest's garments? If you count the number of seeds inside pomegranates grown around the world, they average 613 seeds, which would be symbolic of the number of instructions in the Torah (Law of Moses).

How many male Israelite children were killed in Egypt by Pharaoh's decree? Hopefully, there were not too many that were slain. The midwives feared God and disobeyed Pharaoh. The Lord blessed the midwives, with families of their own, for doing so (Exod. 1:15-21).

Did Peter cut off a Roman soldier's ear with a sword? No, it was Malchus, the slave of the high priest (John 18:10).

Why did they "force" the cross upon Simon the Cyrenian? Passover could only be observed in Jerusalem (Deut. 16:5-8). Simon may have traveled a great distance to be there, and touching an instrument of death would have rendered him unclean for the very occasion he was there for (Matt. 27:32) (Mark 15:21) (Luke 23:26).

What adult got circumcised in the New Testament? Paul circumcised Timothy so he would be a more effective witness to the Jews (Acts 16:3).

What did it mean when the U.S. Senate quoted (Isa. 9:10) to dedicate the ground zero rebuild at the twin towers? Were they knowingly shaking their fist at God? If we read the whole chapter, this is actually a verse about Israel's defiance against God, and His coming judgment upon them for that rebellion.

What is the unpardonable sin? It would be continued, defiant irreverence and unbelief (Matt. 12:22-32) (Mark 3:22-30).

Ode of a Backslider

T'was the night before God came and all through the house,
Not a person was praying, no bride to espouse.
Our Bibles were stored in the closet somewhere,
in hopes that the Word would mature us from there.

The children were dressing to crawl into bed,
Not once ever kneeling or bowing their head.
My old lady in her rocker with babe on her lap,
Were watching the late show while, I took a nap.

When out of the east there arose such a clatter,
I dropped the ashtray trying to see what's the matter?
Spilled beer on the dope as I tripped over the trash,
Hit my head on the shutter, pinched my thumb with the sash.

Even though this is the big party season,
I swore to myself, "There best be a good reason!"
When what to my bloodshot eyes should appear,
But angels proclaiming, "Messiah is here!"

With a trump and a light, sending forth a bright ray,
I knew in a moment, this was surely The Day.
The light of His face made me cover my head,
Yeshua was returning, just like He had said.

And though I possessed worldly wisdom and wealth,
I cried when I saw Him, in spite of myself.
His reward was with Him and His judgment too,
Some ran to hide, while others to Him flew.

The people whose names had been written with love,
had met Him descending in the clouds up above.
Those who were ready; rose with great joyous sound,
while the rest of us were left just standing around.

In the book of life that He held in His hand,
was written the name of every saved man.
He spoke not a word as He searched for my name,
When He said "it's not here," my head hung in shame.

When asked if I had run a good race,
There was no way I could look in His face.
My account held little of which I could tell,
I shook like a leaf as His voice boomed out, "Well...?"

I fell to my knees, but it was too late,
I had waited too long, thus sealing my fate.
I was weeping and gnashing when cast out of sight,
If only I, and mine had been ready tonight.

In the words of this poem the meaning is clear,
The return of the Lord draws ever so near.
There is only one life and come the last call,
We'll know that God's Word was true after all.

As we journey through these lives from birth to our grave,
Let us realize we will never have it made.
We will never really get there or find total relaxation,
Unless we understand life's journey "is" our destination.

In twenty four hours, now will be yesterday,
What will you look back on; did you walk in His Way?

Bibliography

Appleman, Hyman "Antichrist and the Jews" 1950, Zondervan

Bailey, Cyril "The Legacy of Rome" 1923, Clarendon Press

Benson, George Willard "The Cross, Its History and Symbolism" 1934, Hacker

Blackstone, William E. "Jesus is Coming" 1932, Revell Co.

Blavatsky, H. P. "Isis Unveiled" 1923, Theosophical Publishing

Boettner, Loraine "The Millennium" 1957; "Roman Catholicism" 1962, Presbyterian and Reformed Publishing Co.

Bower, Archibald "History of the Popes" 1845, Griffith and Simon

Boyd, Frank M. "Ages and Dispensations" 1955, Gospel Publishing House

Bray, John L. "The Origin of the Pre-Tribulation Rapture Teaching" 1982, John L. Bray Ministry Inc.

Broderick, Robert C. "Concise Catholic Dictionary" 1944, The Bruce Publishing Co.

Bryant, Alton T. "The New Compact Bible Dictionary" 1967, Zondervan Publishing House

Bury, J. B. "The Cambridge Ancient History, Egypt and Babylonia" 1924, The Macmillan Co.

Chiniquy, Charles "Fifty Years in the Church of Rome" 1953, Christ's Mission

Clarke, Adam "Clarke's Commentary" Abingdon Press

"Collier's Encyclopedia" 1983, Macmillan Educational Co.

Cox, William E. "Biblical Studies in Final Things" 1966, Presbyterian and Reformed Publishing Co.

Cumont, Franz "The Mysteries of Mithra" 1956, Dover Publications

D'Aubigne, J. H. "History of the Reformation" 1872, Putnam

DeHaan, M. R. "The Second Coming of Jesus" 1997, Kregel Classics

Doane, T. W. "Bible Myths" 1928, J. W. Bouton

"Eerdman's Concise Bible Handbook" 1973, Lion Publishing

"Encyclopedia of Religion and Ethics" 1922, James Hastings

"Encyclopedia Judaica" 1972, Keter Publishing House

Fausset, A. R. "Expository Bible Encyclopedia" Zondervan

Flick, Alexander C. "The Decline of the Medieval Church" 1930, Knopf

Ford, Herschel W. "Seven Simple Sermons on the Second Coming" 1946, Zondervan

Forlong, J. G. R. "Encyclopedia of Religions" 1964, University Books

Fortman, Edmund J. "The Triune God" 1972, Baker Book House

Freeman, James M. "Manners and Customs of the Bible" 1972, Logos International

Graves, Robert Brent "The God of Two Testaments" 1977, Hazelwood, Mo.

"Grolier Encyclopedia of Knowledge" 1995, Grolier Inc.

Halley, Henry H. "Halley's Bible Handbook" 1927, Zondervan Publishing House

Harris, R. Laird "Theological Wordbook of the Old Testament" 1980, Moody press

Hastings, James "Hastings Encyclopedia of Religion and Ethics" 1928, Charles Scribner's Sons

Hefele, Karl Joseph "A History of the Councils of the Church" 1883, Edinburgh, T. T. Clark

Hislop, Alexander "The Two Babylons" 1853, 1959, Loizeaux Brothers Inc.

"Illustrated Bible Dictionary" 1980, Tyndale House Publishers

Inman, Thomas "Ancient Pagan and Modern Christian Symbolism" 1874, Bristol

"International Standard Bible Encyclopedia" 1946, Eerdmans

Ironside, H.A. "Isaiah" 1952; "Daniel" 1911; "Revelation" 1920; Loizeaux Brothers Inc.

Josephus, Flavius "The Complete Works of Josephus" 1960, Porter and Coates

Kertzer, David "The Popes against the Jews" 2001, Alfred Knopf

Kimball, William R. "The Rapture, a Question of Timing" 1985, Baker Book House

Ladd, George E. "The Blessed Hope" 1956, Eerdmans

Layard, Austen Henry "Ninevah and its Remains" 1849, Putnam

Lindsey, Hal "The Late Great Planet Earth" 1970; "Satan is alive and well on Planet Earth" 1972, Zondervan

Lohse, Bernard "A Short History of Christian Doctrine" 1966, Philadelphia Fortress Press

MacPherson, David "The Great Rapture Hoax" 1983, New Puritan Library

Mauro, Phillip "The Seventy Weeks and the Great Tribulation" 1944, Reiner Publications

M'Clintock, John and Strong, James "Biblical, Theological and Ecclesiastical Cyclopedia" 1894, Harper and Brothers

Miller and Miller "Harper's Bible Dictionary" 1959, Harper and Brothers

Nichols, Robert Hastings "The Growth of the Christian Church" 1941, Westminster Press

Orr, William W. "Antichrist, Armageddon and the End of the World" 1966, Dunham Publishing Company

"Oxford Companion to the Bible" 1985

Richards, Lawrence O. "The Bible Reader's Companion" 1991, Ottenheimer Publishers Inc.

Ridpath, John Clarke "Ridpath's History of the World" 1912, Jones Publishing Co.

Roth, Cecil "History of the Jews" 1954, Schocken Books Inc.

Russell, J. Stuart "The Parousia" 1983, Baker Book House

Schaff, Philip "History of the Christian Church" 1960, Eerdmans

Scofield, C. I. "Scofield Reference Bible KJV" 1909, Oxford University Press

Scott, C. Anderson "Romanism and the Gospel" 1946, Westminster Press

Seldes, George "The Vatican; Yesterday, Today, Tomorrow" 1934, Harper and Brothers

Seymour, William Wood "The Cross in Tradition, History and Art" 1897, G. P. Putnam and Sons

Silver, Jesse F. "The Lord's Return" 1914, Revell

Smith, William "A Dictionary of the Bible" 1948, MacDonald Publishing Company

Strong, James "Strong's Concordance of the Bible KJV" 1947, Abingdon Press

"American Journal of Semitic Language and literature" 1905

"The Catholic Encyclopedia" 1911, Robert Appleton Co.

"The Encyclopedia Americana" 1956, Grolier Inc.

"The Encyclopedia of Religions" 1987, Macmillan Publishing

"The Jerome Biblical Commentary" 1968, Prentice-Hall

"The Jewish Encyclopedia" 1901, Funk and Wagnalls Co.

"The New Catholic Encyclopedia" 1967, McGraw-Hill

"The New Encyclopedia Britannica" 1985, Henry G. Allen Co.

"The New International Dictionary of New Testament Theology" 1976, Zondervan Publishing House

"The Popular and Critical Bible Encyclopedia" 1901, The Howard Severance Company

"The Pulpit Commentary" 1950, Eerdman's Publishing Co.

Unger, Merrill F. "Unger's Bible Dictionary" 1981, Moody Press

"The Volume Library" 1929, Educators Association

"Vatican 2 Council Decisions" Public Library Edition

Vine, W. E. "An Expository Dictionary of New Testament Words" 1940, Revell

Walsh, Mary E. "The Wine of Roman Babylon" 1945, Southern Publishing Association

Weigall, Arthur "The Paganism in our Christianity" 1928, G. P. Putnam and Sons

Weymouth, Richard Francis "The New Testament in Modern Speech" 1929, Harper and Brothers

Whitcomb, John and Morris, Henry "The Genesis Flood" 1973, Baker Book House

Wilder, John P. "The Other Side of Rome" 1959, Zondervan

Williams, Henry Smith "The Historian's History of the World" 1907, The History Association

Willmington, H. L. "The King is Coming" 1997, Tyndale House

Woodrow, Ralph "Great Prophecies of the Bible" 1971; "His Truth is Marching On" 1977; "Amazing Discoveries" 1979; "Noah's Flood, Joshua's Long Day and Lucifer's Fall" 1984; Ralph Woodrow Evangelistic Association Inc.

"World Book Encyclopedia" 1965, World Book Inc.

Wright, Charles H. H. "Cruden's Handy Concordance" 1963, Zondervan Publishing House

Young, Robert "Analytical Concordance to the Bible KJV" 1964, Wm. B. Eerdmans Publishing Company